CHICK

His Unpublished Memoirs and the Memories of Those Who Knew Him

MW01005614

CHICK

*His Unpublished Memoirs
and the Memories
of Those Who Knew Him*

CHICK HEARN

and

STEVE SPRINGER

TRIUMPH
BOOKS
CHICAGO

Library of Congress Cataloging-in-Publication Data

Hearn, Chick.
    Chick : his unpublished memoirs and the memories of those who knew him / Chick Hearn and Steve Springer.
        p. cm.
    ISBN 1-57243-618-2
        1. Hearn, Chick. 2. Sportscasters—United States—Anecdotes. I. Hearn, Chick. II. Title.

GV742.42.H46S67 2004
796'.092—dc22

                                                                    2004044027

This book is available in quantity at special discounts for your group or organization. For further information, contact:
Triumph Books
601 South LaSalle Street
Suite 500
Chicago, Illinois 60605
(312) 939-3330
Fax (312) 663-3557

Printed in U.S.A.
ISBN 1-57243-618-2
Design by Patricia Frey
All photos courtesy of the Hearn family unless indicated otherwise.

This book is dedicated to Fran, my wondrous husband of nearly 64 years, our son Gary, our daughter Samantha, and my lifelines now that they are gone: granddaughter Shannon Hearn-Newman, Louie Newman, and my great-granddaughter Kayla.

And I can't forget the boys, Oliver and Ashley, our two little Bichons.

Troubles can strengthen you. I started looking outside myself for that strength, but I found out it really comes from within. I guess it's been there all along.

Fran's dedication to his dream of being a sports broadcaster will sustain me, knowing he loved every minute of his career with a passion.

I hope, through this book, you will learn more about Fran as a person, the Fran I knew away from the microphone. He had a great sense of humor and always took the time to laugh, to love, and to smell the roses.

He loved us all more than the air he breathed.

The silence is still deafening, but I know they're all in heaven now, my whole loving family.

—Marge Hearn

Contents

Foreword

In 1960, the then–Minneapolis Lakers were moved to Los Angeles. We were the team that made the back pages of the local newspapers. The Rams and the Dodgers were the headliners in Los Angeles' sports world.

But soon, Chick Hearn changed the perception of professional basketball in L.A. His word's-eye view of Laker games made fans realize that they had the most gifted and unique announcer in all of the NBA. The Lakers today are the most popular professional team in Los Angeles, and, some would argue, in all of sports. That's thanks in great part to Chick's enormous popularity and his way with words. When Chick was only on radio, people would turn the sound down on their televisions to hear him.

All seven Lakers in the Hall of Fame—Baylor, Chamberlain, Goodrich, Magic, Kareem, Worthy, and myself—were made bigger than life by Chick. It's fitting that Chick was inducted into the Hall himself in 2003 because, if not for him, some of the rest of us might not have made it. He did the same job of legend-building for the two Lakers in the waiting room of the Hall: Shaquille and Kobe.

Chick made Laker games a part of the culture of Southern California for many generations, millions of fans. His many Chickisms will forever remain a part of basketball's vernacular.

His streak of 3,338 consecutive games announced is amazing. Chick was the Laker play-by-play man through the sixties, the seventies, the eighties, the nineties, and into the new century. His work ethic was just incredible. When he started announcing, JFK was president. He saw nine presidents in the White House over the span of his fantastic career. He saw people in space. He saw men on the moon. He announced through the hippie era and the yuppie era. He saw styles come and go: thin ties, wide ties, short skirts, and skirts to the knees. So many changes in our country and in the world, yet one thing remained the same: Chick Hearn announcing basketball.

Chick always talked about the importance of being objective when he worked, but he was the most biased unbiased man I've known when it came to the Lakers. He was the heart of the Lakers. Yet despite his deep feelings for the team, Chick was also the most professional man I've ever known.

He was truly a genius and a treasure for the city of Los Angeles, yet he had the ability to make everyone he came in contact with feel important. He had a common appeal that stretched across all levels of society. It's impossible for me to believe we will ever again see someone have such a profound effect on Los Angeles.

Chick played an extremely important role in my life over 40 years, but I cherished him most as a friend and confidant.

We will all sorely miss him.

—Jerry West

Acknowledgments

It was a voice so rich, so powerful, so memorable that it held the fascination of three generations of Lakers fans, the only play-by-play voice the team had for 42 years, the only voice it needed.

To tell the story of the man behind the voice, the story of Chick Hearn, it took 105 voices in addition to his own. And given unlimited time and space, this oral history could have been expanded to include 105 more.

Everyone, it seems, has a Chick Hearn story.

Normally, when you interview this many people on any subject, the material becomes repetitious, with one story starting to sound like another. But not in this case. Hearn had so many facets to his career and his life that each person's experience was unique.

So thank you to each of the 104 others who have added to my own memories of Chick. They are: J. A. Adande, Lucius Allen, Bob Baker, Elgin Baylor, Howard Beck, Sheron Bellio, Bill Bertka, Steve Bisheff, Alison Bogli, Kobe Bryant, Larry Burnett, Jeanie Buss, Jerry Buss, Dyan Cannon, Steve Chase, Mitch Chortkoff, Dennis Cypher, Bill Dwyre, Roy Englebrecht, Keith Erickson, Roy Firestone, Derek Fisher, Rick Fox, Ray Gasper, Joel Glass, Brian Golden, Robert Goulet, Curt Gowdy, Shirley Gruber, Harold Guyer, Del Harris, Steve Hartman, Marge Hearn, Jim Hill, Rod Hundley, John Ireland, Gary James, Jaime Jarrin, Magic Johnson, Bob Keisser, Tom Kelly, Sandy Kessler, Mitch Kupchak, Stu Lantz, Ralph Lawler, Don Lechman, Randy Levitz, Mary Lou Liebich, Steve Lombardo, Isaac Lowenkron, Bill MacDonald, Dick Manoogian, Joe McDonnell, Tricia Maloney, Penny Marshall, Alan Massengale, Larry Merchant, Al Michaels, Bob Miller, Jeffrey Moualim, John Nadel, Stu

Nahan, Shannon Hearn-Newman, Pat O'Brien, Shaquille O'Neal, Frank O'Neill, Scott Ostler, Ross Porter, Kurt Rambis, Linda Rambis, Joe Resnick, Pat Riley, Lon Rosen, Josh Rosenfeld, Michael Roth, Claire Rothman, Curt Sandoval, Fred Schaus, Vin Scully, Lynn Shackelford, Bill Sharman, T. J. Simers, Jo Skibby, Bob Speck, Ray Stallone, Bob Steiner, Larry Stewart, Susan Stratton, Paul Sunderland, Lawrence Tanter, Mychal Thompson, Michael Ventre, Gary Vitti, Mark Walch, Bill Walton, Jerry West, Johnny West, Paul Westhead, Cathy Whittaker, Pat Williams, Tex Winter, James Worthy, Chris Zearing, and Lee Zeidman.

Behind the voices are so many who made this book and CD a reality.

Thank you Lon Rosen for putting this deal together, as only you can.

Thank you Al Michaels for lending your own powerful voice to provide the CD narration.

Thank you Jack Nicholson and your representative, Bob Colbert, for allowing us to share your feelings about Chick.

Thank you Tom Bast and Mitchell Rogatz for believing in this project and making it a Triumph book.

Thank you Kelley Thornton for your meticulous editing, Linc Wonham for laying out the photos, and Blythe Hurley and all the other unseen faces at Triumph for bringing the whole process together.

Thank you NBA for allowing Chick's unrivaled broadcasts to be heard once again.

Thank you Jerry West and Bill Walton for your special contributions.

Thank you Dave Blume and Dave Gillerman for allowing fans to once again enjoy Chick the rapster.

Thank you Joe Garner, whose creative mind turned the merging of books with CDs into a best-selling phenomenon, and for being there as a friend to lean on.

Thank you Richard Kaufman for your crucial help at a critical moment.

Thank you Henry Schipper for providing the script and the expertise that resulted in a moving, exhilarating CD, and thank you Mike Forslund for providing the engineering.

Thank you to Susan Stratton and all the other folks at KCAL, Channel 9, who help to keep alive the memory of the man whose voice and image graced your airwaves for so long. Jeff Proctor, Scott Henry, Alan Massengale, Garry Ashton, Tom Mouzis, Russell Kodani, and Bobby Matthews, thank you all.

Thank you Harry Abrams, Chick's agent, Brad Parton, his financial advisor, and Lou Baumeister, former president of California Sports, for always being there for him.

Thank you Dina and Daniel for providing me, in my moments of fatigue, with inspiration by the example of how you live your lives daily.

Thank you Annette for just being there. As Chick had Marge to sustain him through all of the years, I have been blessed to have you.

And finally, thank you Alan Springer, my son, who spent many an all-nighter turning old, dusty tapes from the vault into a CD that will forever be a living memorial to Chick. You've come a long way since you turned the closet in your room into a studio, watching Lakers games with the sound turned down while playing make-believe Chick Hearn into your little tape recorder. At 25, I know you have many exciting years ahead in which you will create countless memories of your own in this business.

—Steve Springer

Introduction

As his eyes scanned the list of proposed chapter headings for his autobiography spread before him in the spacious living room of his Encino home, Chick Hearn suddenly became aware of someone looking over his shoulder.

"What are you doing?" he asked, that mischievous look in his eyes as he turned to Marge, his wife of 63 years.

"I want to see what it looks like," she said.

"You'll have to wait and buy the book," said Chick. "That way, at least I know I'll sell one copy."

He was kidding. But not really.

It took me several years to convince Chick to write his memoirs. He kept saying the fans didn't care what he thought. They cared about the players.

Who, he wanted to know, would buy a book about Chick Hearn?

The better question would be, who wouldn't?

Chick's career encompassed nearly the entire history of the Lakers since their arrival in Los Angeles, having begun his unprecedented time behind the microphone for this storied franchise in the spring of 1961, starting in the second playoff series of their first season in L.A.

He taught the city pro basketball. He was the voice of the Lakers for 42 seasons, including an unprecedented 3,338 straight games. He saw the Lakers win nine championships, including a three-peat. He did the play-by-play for a Laker team that set a record for the ages with 33 victories in a row. Chick was there for West and Baylor. He was there for Magic and Kareem. And he was there for Shaq and Kobe. He worked for owners Bob Short, Jack Kent Cooke, and Jerry Buss. He provided a word's-eye view of all those heartbreaking losses to the Boston Celtics in the NBA Finals of the sixties and those euphoric triumphs over the Celtics in the eighties.

With a story about every player who ever wore the purple and gold, and a memory about every important game the Lakers ever played, Chick was an irreplaceable storehouse of facts, anecdotes, and quotes. It would have been a shame if he had never had the chance to tell his story. Unfortunately, he only had the opportunity to tell part of it before death claimed him at age 85 on August 5, 2002.

What follows, preserved for all time, is the completed portion of a book we had been working on. Here is Chick's word's-eye view of his own life, supplemented by the memories of so many whose lives he touched, from the players on the court, to the fans in the seats, to all those who shared those endless but unforgettable road trips. There are also contributions from the color men, producers, and statisticians who contributed to those wonderful broadcasts. Interspersed throughout the book, in a sans serif typeface, are my own memories and observations.

This is Chick's story at last.

Long overdue.

—Steve Springer

~ 1 ~
His Stories

Before his death, Chick Hearn began work on his autobiography. What follows in this chapter and in parts of succeeding chapters is Chick's story from his word's-eye view.

CHICK

Books, books, books. So many times, in so many cities, on so many road trips over the years, I would pass a bookstore, look in the window, and there would be a book on the Lakers.

This team could have its own library.

Wilt wrote a book. Kareem had several. So did Riles. Magic had a bunch. Even sportswriters like Steve Springer, Scott Ostler, and Roland Lazenby did Laker books.

They all had their say. Springer has finally convinced me I should have mine.

I've been here since the end of the team's first season in L.A. But a play-by-play broadcast allows only so much time for storytelling. Over the years, the excess material has been piling up.

So here is the best of it.

The Owner in the Suite
Basketball is a game of shots and rebounds, slam dunks and dribble drives, games going in the refrigerator, and teams, including the Lakers on occasion, going in the tank.

But for me, the best part of basketball is the people. I've been fortunate enough to meet so many wonderful, unforgettable characters in this game.

But none was as unforgettable as Jack Kent Cooke, who was my boss in the years he owned the team, and my friend always.

Still, if he felt he needed to take action on behalf of his beloved Lakers, he never let our friendship stand in the way.

One time, Jerry West, while still a player, had a disagreement with Mr. Cooke during the off-season over Jerry's contract. It got so bad, they refused to talk to each other, which left me right where I didn't want to be—in the middle.

I got a call from Rosemary Garmand, Mr. Cooke's secretary. "Mr. Cooke wants you to find Jerry West," she said, "and get him to the office as quickly as you can."

"I don't know where Jerry West is," I told her. "I haven't seen him in two weeks."

"Well, Mr. Cooke wants you to find him," she insisted.

I knew darn well where Jerry was—out on the golf course. When I finally got ahold of him, I told him, "Jerry, I'm in a spot. Cooke said you've got to come out to the Forum."

"Damn it," West said. "I'm not going to the Forum."

Well, I relayed that message to Rosemary. A few minutes later, Mr. Cooke himself called. "You go over to the golf course," he told me in no uncertain terms, "you get him by the arm, you put him in the car, and you bring him here."

Now I was mad. "I don't have to take this," I said. "I quit." And I hung up.

The phone immediately rang again. Again, it was Mr. Cooke. "You can't quit," he said.

"No, I can't," I agreed, "and I can't bring Jerry West over there, either."

Under Mr. Cooke, I was elevated in the organization, adding the title of assistant general manager to my broadcasting duties.

I was serving in that capacity in 1975 when the Lakers, hoping to find another force in the middle to replace Wilt Chamberlain, who had retired, were deciding between Kareem Abdul-Jabbar and Bill Walton.

Which one to pursue? I went to a team meeting on the subject, being led, of course, by Mr. Cooke.

Figuring that Kareem was five and a half years older, I said, "I vote to go after Walton."

"What do you mean you vote for Walton?" asked Mr. Cooke. "The rest of us have agreed on Kareem."

"Then why did you ask me?" I said.

"Because," replied Mr. Cooke, "you have the right to vote."

A Body in the Room

Road trips were always an adventure with the Lakers and not necessarily just because of what happened on the court.

I remember one year, when the Lakers were in Baltimore to play the Bullets, a maid cleaning the block of rooms assigned to our club made a shocking discovery. She knocked on the door of one of those rooms, but nobody answered. So, she went in, and there, on the floor, she discovered a body. Terrified, she called a security officer, who immediately phoned Fred Schaus, then the Laker coach.

"Mr. Schaus," he was told, "one of your people is unconscious on the floor in one of your rooms. We don't know how serious it is."

Schaus' reaction?

He yelled, "Oh boy, I just hope it isn't West or Baylor."

It wasn't, just some silly sportswriter who had had too much to drink.

A Figure in the Air

Speaking of Elgin Baylor, he was one of the best basketball players I ever saw. The gravity-defying feats that Dr. J and Michael Jordan later performed, drawing worldwide attention as the NBA became a global sport, were being done by Baylor 20 years earlier, when Julius Erving was still dribbling on a grammar school playground and Jordan hadn't even been born yet. Hanging in the air, Baylor was an offensive machine with enough gears to put the greatest defenders who ever lived in the popcorn machine.

The first time I ever met Baylor was before a USC football game I was broadcasting for CBS Radio at the University of Washington in Seattle. I attended a luncheon at Seattle University, where Baylor played. Afterward, his coach, John Castellani, came up, introduced himself, and invited me to come watch Baylor practice.

We drove over to this old, dilapidated building on the campus, walked in a little door, and there, sitting with his legs sprawled out— about 20 feet long it seemed—was Elgin Baylor.

He looked up and said, "Coach, I can't practice today. My back is feeling miserable." Coach said to him, "That's too bad, Elgin. I want you to meet Chick Hearn, CBS Radio, Los Angeles."

With that, Baylor jumped to his feet and announced, "I'm going to get my stuff on."

He disappeared, reappeared minutes later in his uniform, and proceeded to disappear into the rafters of the gym, putting on an aerial show like nothing I had ever seen before.

But I saw it again and again during my years with the Lakers.

One of the best games I ever broadcast was in Philadelphia in 1961. Baylor had held the league's single-game scoring record with 71 points, accomplished against the Knicks in Madison Square Garden the season before. The game between the Lakers and Philadelphia went into three overtimes, with Wilt Chamberlain, playing for Philly, winding up with 78 points to break Baylor's record.

I went to Baylor after the game and told him, "It hardly seems fair, because Wilt had a lot more minutes to play with because of the three overtimes."

Baylor took a puff on a cigarette, looked at me, and replied, "Don't worry about it. One day, the big fellow will make a hundred."

Less than three months later, in Hershey, Pennsylvania, Wilt indeed scored 100 points in a single game.

Elgin didn't need much coaching to come up with a great play on the court or a great line off the hardwood.

After interviewing Elgin on live TV one time, I wound up the segment with the standard close: "Elgin, for being with us, take this gift certificate to any Harris & Frank men's store and get yourself a nice suit."

On camera, Elgin looked me over from head to toe, looked at the gift certificate, then handed it back and said, "Here, Chick, you need this more than I do."

A Clock in His Head

I called him Mr. Clutch. And I always said Jerry West must have had a clock in his head. That's the only way he could have excelled at what I called "nervous time."

I saw it so many times in my years with the team: clock running down, Lakers behind, ball goes into West's hands. Could be backcourt, midcourt, or frontcourt. Could be 30 seconds left, 10 seconds, tenths of a second. Could be Celtics, Knicks, or 76ers. Could be single, double, or triple coverage, whatever the officials would allow in those frantic, final ticks of the clock. Didn't matter. West was going to find a way to get that ball in the air and give his team a chance to win.

One of the first times I remember seeing West weave his magic was back when Earvin Johnson was still a Lansing, Michigan, toddler. It was Game 3 of the 1962 NBA Finals between the Lakers and the Celtics. A then-record Laker crowd of 15,180 had come to the Los Angeles Sports Arena to see what figured to be a pivotal game in a series that was tied at 1–1.

It was West who hit a jumper and then two free throws to even the score at 115 with four seconds remaining.

On the in-bounds pass, Boston's Sam Jones tried to get the ball to Bob Cousy—a wise choice since Cousy was the most sure-handed of guards.

But instead, another sure-handed guard named West intercepted the ball. As he controlled it in his hands, he stood approximately 35 feet from the Laker basket.

There were three seconds left.

With an open court, West had a decision to make: shoot a jumper or try to traverse the 35 feet of hardwood to get the guaranteed layup.

West took off, going for the layup. And darned if he didn't make it, giving the Lakers their most memorable victory of their two seasons in L.A.

Red Auerbach, then the Boston coach, said it was impossible to dribble nearly half the court and make that basket in three seconds. So he got the film of the game, ran that play a thousand times, and it always came out the same: 2.9 seconds.

In those days, arena clocks didn't show tenths of a second the way they do today. But, obviously, the clock in West's head did.

There was, of course, the quintessential clock-beating moment by West during the 1970 NBA Finals between the Lakers and the Knicks. It was in Game 3 at the Forum, with the series tied at a game apiece.

Dave DeBusschere had hit a jumper to put New York ahead by 2 with three seconds to play.

With no timeouts for the Lakers, Chamberlain grabbed the ball when it came through the hoop and flipped it to West, who was still in the backcourt. West went into a three-step dribble drive, but he knew there would be no clutch layup. Not this time. Not from the backcourt with the clock in his brain telling him time had just about run out.

So West took the only option left to him—a desperation heave of approximately 60 feet. Willis Reed leaped up in front of West and damn near blocked it. That was stupid of Reed because, if he'd committed a foul, it would have been three-to-make-two for West.

Instead, West got his 2 in a nearly impossible fashion. Incredibly, that 60-foot heave went in.

Any Laker fan who was around in those days remembers that shot. What I remember is that when Chamberlain grabbed the ball after the DeBusschere basket, he never went out of bounds before throwing it in. The film clearly shows that and shows that a ref was looking right at him. The play could have been whistled dead right there.

Instead, West made a shot for the ages. When the ball went through, one of the Knicks—I never did figure out who it was—fell flat on his back, as if in a dead faint, under the basket.

Chamberlain thought the Lakers had won. They had to go to the locker room to get him back for the overtime.

If West hit that shot today, of course, it would be a game-winner with the three-point rule in effect.

You wouldn't believe that the Lakers could lose a game like that after such an inspirational moment by West, but they found a way: New York won in overtime, 111–108.

I also remember another Jerry West, one most folks never saw. That was Jerry West the rookie, back in our first season in L.A. If you can believe it, he was our gopher at card games on the road. Poor Jerry—he'd have to go for the sandwiches and the pop. He couldn't afford to play in those card games anyway. He only made $15,000 that first season.

A Giant in the Game

Wilt Chamberlain was a wonderful player who took a bad rap for not winning enough championships. He was the strongest man I had ever seen and could just dominate a game.

He could tell you before the season what department he was going to lead the league in, and then he'd go out and make good on his prediction. One season, he told me, "I'm going to lead the league in assists."

I told him, "You're crazy; no center has ever led the league in assists."

He did.

Chamberlain averaged a little over 50 points per game one season. He averaged 48 minutes plus per game that same season, 1961–1962.

But not everybody thought he was so wonderful. When Bill van Breda Kolff was the Laker coach, he and Chamberlain didn't always get along. One of the things that disturbed van Breda Kolff was that Chamberlain often had a chicken in hand to eat when he entered the locker room before a game.

Schaus, then the Laker general manager, told Chamberlain not to do that anymore, which didn't go over too well with him.

Well, the next game, Schaus and van Breda Kolff got to the locker room, and there was Chamberlain, munching away on hot dogs. He had a dozen with him.

"Nobody said anything about hot dogs," Chamberlain announced.

Riles in the Rain

My relationship with Pat Riley was unique. I watched him as a player, both with the Lakers and with other teams. I worked with him as my broadcast partner. I talked to him about the pros and cons of coaching when he came to me for advice after coach Paul Westhead asked him to be his assistant. And, of course, I was there for all of Riley's years as the Laker head coach.

Those years caused me all sorts of agony. I loved the guy, but I wish he could have figured out someplace else to stand during games instead of directly in front of me. It was no problem at the Forum, where I sat halfway up in the stands, my view unobstructed. But on the road, where I was usually courtside right by the Laker bench, I would get a stiff neck trying to see around Riley. He seemed to move around that sideline as much as he did on the court in his playing days. The more tense the situation, the more Riley moved, crouched, and generally blocked me out. Others may have criticized Phil Jackson for staying put on the bench much of the game, but I loved him for it.

The moment I remember most from Riley's playing days was after a preseason game between the Lakers and the Trail Blazers in Portland in 1970.

After beginning his professional career with the then–San Diego Rockets, Riley was picked by the Trail Blazers in the expansion draft leading up to their first season, but he wanted no part of that team.

It had been raining heavily the night of that Laker–Trail Blazers exhibition game, so, when I bumped into Riley outside the arena afterward, he was soaked, with water dripping from that famous head of hair. His mood matched the weather. He was already tired of Portland.

"Chick," he told me, "you've got to get me out of here."

I put in a word for him and, sure enough, a deal was almost immediately worked out, the Lakers claiming him on waivers.

Riley spent the next five seasons as a Laker on the court, and eventually moved up the ladder to become the team's most successful coach, a distinction currently being challenged by Phil Jackson.

A Character in the Locker Room

Laker characters? Where do I begin? Probably the end is as good a place as any—the end of the 1962 NBA Finals between the Lakers and the Celtics.

That one ended like all others between those two teams from 1959 through 1984: with Red Auerbach lighting up that ever-present cigar and the Lakers smoldering.

But this one may have been the worst because the Lakers' Frank Selvy had a chance to win it all at the end of regulation play of the seventh game with a 15-foot baseline jumper. Now Selvy wasn't exactly your Aunt Minnie when it came to shooting a basketball. As a matter of fact, playing for Furman University, he once scored 100 points in a game, just like Chamberlain did in the pros. But Selvy missed that 15-footer—I can still see it—and the Lakers lost in overtime.

That was the second of eight straight Laker defeats at the hands of Boston in the Finals. I've often thought that if Selvy had made that shot, maybe it all would have been different. Maybe the Lakers would have gained the confidence they needed against the Celtics. Maybe the Lakers would have gone on and done pretty well against them in some of those other Finals series.

But then again, considering Boston had Bill Russell at center, maybe not.

I can assure you of one thing. If Russell had been a Laker in the six NBA Finals between the two clubs for which he played, the Lakers would have won them all.

But I digress. The point of this story is Laker center Ray Felix. In the locker room after the Lakers lost in overtime in '62, a few tears began to form in the eyes of a few players.

So Ray stood up—now remember, they had just lost the seventh and deciding game—and said in a loud voice, "Don't worry, we're going to get them tomorrow."

Ray said a lot of things that left you shaking your head.

One time against Russell, probably the greatest defender the game has ever known, Felix had four straight shots blocked. Keep in mind, Felix was 6'11", Russell 6'10". It didn't matter. This was Russell.

The stubborn but overmatched Felix moved in again against Russell, faked one way, and then went the other to put up a fifth shot. Russell couldn't get it. Nobody could. It sailed over the basket, over the backboard, and into the seats.

Felix grinned at Russell and said, "You didn't get that one, baby."

Losing It on the Floor

The Lakers had a guard named Flynn Robinson who went on a dribble drive in one game that still gets me laughing hysterically every time I think about it.

I don't think his teammates knew, and I certainly didn't, that Robinson wore a hairpiece.

He had the ball, he had an open lane to the basket, and he had it in full gear. But just about the time he crossed midcourt, apparently, the glue loosened on the front of the toupée. That wig blew backward and stood straight up, looking like the bill of a cap.

No problem. Robinson just kept going and made the shot.

How I was able to describe it through the laughter, I'll never know.

Then there was Johnny Neumann, another Laker guard, who was told to go into a game and responded by yanking off his sweats only to discover he'd forgotten to put on his shorts.

He got the biggest ovation of his career.

And there was Dick Barnett, still another Laker guard, who was also captain of our "All-Flaker team" one season. He got mad the second season. They took his captaincy away. He was really something.

Barnett was dribbling down the floor one night in San Diego when the Clippers still played there at the Sports Arena. I worked courtside in that building, sitting at a press table.

A defender pushed Barnett as he came upcourt, shoving him onto the table and causing him to knock over a phone and cut himself.

Looking down at his elbow as he tried to recover, Barnett saw blood. He picked up the loose phone—the game was still going on—yelled, "Get me a doc," hung the phone up, and then ran back onto the court and right back into the flow of the game.

That got him the captain's job back among the "All-Flakers."

A Jester on the Court

"Hot" Rod Hundley is best known for his searing wit and excellent presence behind the mike. Those are certainly qualities I appreciated in him when he was my broadcast partner and entertaining traveling companion.

Some people have forgotten that he was a pretty good basketball player himself, first at West Virginia and then with the Lakers. It's understandable how they'd forget. Hundley was followed from West Virginia to the Lakers by another guard, named Jerry West. Hundley was good, but not that good. But even in his playing days, Hundley was always good with that wit.

He was on that 1961–1962 squad that came within 15 feet of beating Boston in the Finals.

In the locker room after the game, Hundley came up to poor Selvy, who had missed that crucial shot, leaned over, and told Selvy in that soft, syrupy voice of his, "It could happen to anybody. Don't worry. You only cost us about $30,000."

And Hundley wasn't done yet. Not for years.

Long after both men had retired, Hundley would call Selvy at home when he knew his former teammate wasn't there and would always leave the same message on Selvy's answering machine: "Nice shot."

Hundley was in uniform the night Baylor set the NBA scoring record in New York with 71 points. Afterward, he and Baylor hopped in a cab to check out the sights in Manhattan.

"Be careful," Hundley told the driver. "You've got 73 points in this cab."

A Seat in the Stands

One thing fans always want to know is why I don't sit courtside for home games.

When I worked for Mr. Cooke, he insisted that we sit up in the stands so that the seats on the floor could be sold. When Dr. Buss took over the club, he said I could come down on the floor and work if I so desired. He assured me he'd make room for me.

I asked him, "What about the visiting radio and television people?"

"We can't do it for them as well," Dr. Buss said, "because there would be too many."

So I told him, "No, I can't do that to my fellow broadcasters. I'll stay up where I am."

Half Nelson and a Slam Dunk at the Airport

When you looked at Rudy LaRusso, your first inclination was certainly not to laugh. Especially if you were lining up against him in the front court. LaRusso was a tough forward. It was because of men like him that the term *power forward* was invented. LaRusso wore a no-nonsense expression on the court, and played that way.

But off the court, it was another story. Nobody could make us laugh as easily. Especially when we went to Detroit.

Not the city, just the airport.

You see, they had this stuffed lion at that airport. I don't know what it was for. I guess to entertain the kids.

And LaRusso.

Every time we went through there, that son of a gun would grab that lion, throw it on the floor, fall on top of it, and wrestle ferociously with it. Can you imagine a 6'8" NBA forward wrestling in public with a stuffed lion? People would come running to see what all the fuss was about. Some thought it was a real lion, and some thought LaRusso was just nuts.

Which he was.

I got my own laughs at an airport once, but not intentionally. Marge had knitted me this black-and-white-checkered sweater for some occasion or other, and I kind of liked it. But nobody else seemed to. I took it out of my suitcase at the end of a grueling, two-week trip and took all kinds of heat for it. Everybody seemed to have an insult they only too willingly hurled at that poor sweater.

Finally, when we got to Washington, I'd had enough. Figuring I'd put on a show for everybody, I spotted this poor skycap, a meek little guy lugging bags twice his size. I pulled off the sweater, handed it to him, and waited for him to gush with gratitude.

After carefully examining it—for what, I don't know—he handed the sweater back to me, saying, "I don't want this piece of junk."

Only he didn't use the word *junk*.

I took that sweater and slam dunked it in the nearest trash can.

Hopefully, Marge won't read this.

~ 2 ~
His Roots

CHICK

I assume that anybody reading this book has heard of me, but it's also a pretty safe assumption that nobody reading this book has ever heard of the town I came from.

Not counting relatives, of course, who got complimentary copies.

I was born Francis Dayle Hearn on November 27, 1916, in Buda, Illinois, 133 miles southwest of Chicago. The population of Buda was about 400 when I lived there, and is still under 600.

My father, Frank, came from a farming family in Bradford, 12 miles down the road. My mother, Opal, came from Indiana.

It may surprise people, considering I spent my adult life on hardwood floors, but I never really got the dirt of the farm out of my system. My fondest early memories are of weekend trips back to the family farm in Bradford.

MARGE HEARN

It is easy to figure out who Fran—I know I should call him Chick like everybody else does to avoid confusion, but I've always called him Fran— inherited his wit from. His father was very comical. Fran definitely inherited his height from his mother, Opal, who was 6'. Fran grew to 6'3", helping him to become such a good basketball player in his youth. His father was only about 5'6".

Chick

From the earliest age, Fran was fascinated by basketball. All sports really, but especially basketball.

I remember his mother telling me that, as a little kid, Fran would roll up a pair of socks and shoot them at a door. I suppose he had some mark on that door that served as an imaginary basket, but his mother didn't remember that. All she knew was that he kept shooting those socks at that door.

CHICK

In Buda my dad put his farm overalls away and went to work for the railroad. By the time I was eight, however, Buda was in our rearview mirror, and so were Dad's days with the railroad. We moved to another Illinois town, Aurora, where my father drove a laundry truck.

Our family was growing. My sister, Shirley, was born when I was nine, and my brother, Richard, came along nine years after that. Richard wound up becoming a car salesman in Florida. He sure had the gift of gab. I guess it ran in the family.

Basketball didn't run in our family. I was the only athlete. I played one semester of basketball at Fox Valley High in Aurora. But it was a private school, and there was a tuition fee. When it came time for my second semester, my parents couldn't afford the tuition. So I was asked to leave school.

Turns out, it was the best thing that could have happened to me.

I went to East High in Aurora, where I did OK on the basketball team.

My dad became a huge basketball fan. And a very loud one. I can still see him sitting in the stands screaming at the refs. Somebody should have given him a microphone.

But basketball wasn't the best part of East High. The best part was Marge. That's where I met her.

After all my success on the court, Fox Valley asked me to come back a year later, but there was no way I was giving up East High.

And Marge.

MARGE HEARN

I was one of 11 children of Glen and Bertha Jeffers. I had a lot in common with Fran, who was six months older than I was. We were both heavily into sports in high school. I ran track and also played basketball.

And I couldn't really avoid him. Because our last names were so close in the alphabet and our teachers often sat us alphabetically, I usually wound up right behind him.

But you know, at first I didn't really like him. I thought he was a show-off on the basketball court. I soon realized, however, that's just the way he was. At the high school level, he was kind of like Magic would later be. In his own way, Fran was a showtime player before anyone had ever heard that term.

Besides, he was tall, good-looking, and entertaining, and the other girls liked him, so I figured I'd better hold my tongue.

Because my grades were better than his, I passed him the answers to a lot of tests, especially in English. I have no command of English now, but I did then, and he didn't.

I had told Fran that I was an only child. So for my first date with him, I asked my mother to keep my 10 brothers and sisters in the house.

But when he drove up in that little old Ford of his, they got out and were all over that car like a swarm of bees.

Didn't seem to discourage him.

Everybody around school came to know us as a couple, although, because our lives were so wrapped up in sports, all we ever did was go to games and maybe to a movie once in a while.

They had a "loving cup" at East High. It was given by the graduating seniors to the most lovey-dovey couple in the junior class.

The senior class picked Fran and me to receive that cup. But the night it was presented to us, we got into a big argument on the walk home. I don't remember what the argument was about, but I do remember I got so mad I threw that cup in the bushes.

I figured Fran would go back and find it when things cooled down. But he never did, and I never saw that cup again.

RAY GASPER
High School Friend
Chick and I first met as competitors on the basketball court and remained lifelong friends. He was playing for Saint Mary's grade school, and I was a member of the Saint Joseph's team. We both went on to play for East High.

I still laugh when thinking of the weekend we traveled by bus to play Rockford and Freeport high schools. Chick and I were roommates. There was no way we were going to simply stay in our room and get a good night's sleep, as the coaches demanded.

So there we were at midnight, running up and down the halls, clowning around, knocking on doors to keep the other guys awake, when, all of a sudden, one of the assistant coaches showed up and caught us wearing just our jockey shorts.

––––––––

At East High, Hearn was All-Conference in basketball, honorable mention All-State, and captain of the team in his senior year.

CHICK
After graduating from high school in 1935, I wasn't sure what I wanted to do, but I knew I wanted to stay involved in sports in any way I could.

I went to work for Austin Western, which manufactured farm machinery. The bonus for me was that the job kept me in sports because they had an AAU basketball team. AAU—Amateur Athletic Union—was pretty big in those days. Remember, that was before there was a major pro league. Our team went to Chicago and won the AAU's Central Division title. That qualified us for the AAU national tournament, to be held in Denver.

The day before we were to leave for Denver, on the old CBQ Zephyr train, Austin Western held a luncheon for our team in the company cafeteria. During the Chicago tournament I had been in desperate need of a pair of basketball shoes. The ones I was using had worn down so badly, I was practically playing in my socks. A couple of our boosters noticed and took pity on me, promising me a new pair of shoes. It was either that or keep buying me new socks.

At this luncheon I was presented with a gift-wrapped box. When I ripped off the paper I could see it was a shoebox. I couldn't wait to show off my new footwear, so I stuck my hand in the box with my teammates and everybody else at the luncheon standing around. I was so excited, I didn't notice they were all giggling. Thinking I was pulling out a shoe, I found myself instead holding on to a chicken. A dead, rotting chicken.

My teammates started calling me Chicken, and then Chick. From that dead carcass sprang the name I've carried the rest of my life.

Probably just as well. How many announcers go by the name Fran?

Ray Gasper

Chick worked at one of the Austin Western shop offices while I was a supervisor in the welding department. One day at lunch, we were joined by a fellow employee who was complaining about his straight hair, which he plastered with grease. He wanted to know how Chick and I managed to have such nice, wavy hair.

"We go to a certain beauty parlor downtown," Chick told him, "and get a permanent wave."

This was on a Friday. The following Monday, the guy showed up at work with the most freakish hairdo Chick and I had ever seen.

Chick

While I was happy on the basketball court, I wasn't so happy in the office. I wanted to go out and be a salesman. But my manager told me, "Chick, you go out and start working in the field, that's where you'll still be 20 years from now. At least if you work in the office, you'll have a chance to move up in the company."

He may have been right, but I didn't want to move up in that company. Basketball or no basketball, I wanted out. It was 1937, I had been out of high school two years, and college started to look appealing. Especially because I had a few scholarship offers. Marriage also looked appealing. Marriage with Marge. I scraped together the money for a ring and planned the night I would propose. It was a dream evening. And, as it turned out, a nightmare of a night, even though it was Christmas Eve.

Oh, Marge accepted my proposal—don't ask me why—but just as I was basking in the glow of future matrimony, sitting in the kitchen of my parents' house, harsh reality interceded. The phone rang. It was my mother, calling from a local hospital. My father's laundry truck had slid off an icy road and crashed, seriously injuring him.

There would be no college for me. With my father laid up and an impending marriage, I was going to have to make enough money to support both Marge and my family. My mother planned to do her part and get a job as well, even though she still had two youngsters at home.

On August, 13, 1938, Marge and I were married at St. Mary's Church in Aurora.

I stayed at Austin Western for a few more years, then went to work in Chicago for Dunn and Bradstreet, the business firm. That job was easy. Too easy. I was supposed to go out and meet clients. But I soon realized I could leave the office, make my calls by phone, and have the afternoon off. So I went to the movies every day.

But I wasn't happy. Finally, I told Marge, "If I stay with this job, I'm going to turn out to be a bum."

So I quit that, too.

I took a job as a salesman for a pharmaceutical company and satisfied my ever-present love for sports by refereeing college games.

In 1942 Marge and I had our first child, a son we named Gary. He was the center of our lives for seven months, and then I was separated from both mother and child by the draft board. Like millions of Americans, I went off to serve in World War II, while Marge became a supervisor of 60 kids at an Aurora preschool, allowing her to stay close to Gary while also helping on the home front.

I was proud to do my part for my country, and discovered that my country had returned the favor by opening the door to the path I would follow the rest of my life. Serving in the South Pacific, I was put in special services. I organized a touring military baseball team with our unit in Manila to keep up morale and give everybody a welcome touch of home.

Our team wasn't bad. It went 82–0.

When it was decided that the games were to be broadcast on Armed Forces Radio, they needed a play-by-play announcer. I didn't have any experience, but neither did anybody else on the base. So I was selected for the job, even though I didn't know a darn thing about it. I don't know how much anybody else liked my broadcast, but I didn't want to leave that microphone.

When I got home at the end of the war three years later, I told Marge, "You know, I really liked doing that announcing. I think I'm going to try to get into the business."

Well, I may have liked the industry, but the industry didn't seem to like me. I went to Chicago seeking work as a radio announcer—there wasn't any TV to speak of yet—but came home empty-handed. "Sorry," I was told, "you need a college degree."

I was told the same thing in Aurora, until a little station with the call letters WMRO finally agreed to take a chance on me. I didn't care how little it was. Announcing was what I wanted to do, and, with Marge's blessings, that was what I was going to do.

My father wasn't so convinced. I can still recall him looking me in the eye and asking me, "Do you really think radio is here to stay?"

It wasn't exactly sitting at Staples Center and broadcasting the NBA Finals. I did sports at WMRO, yes, but I also did news, religious programming, and everything else except sweep the floor. And I would have done that, too, to hang onto my job, even though it only paid $25 per week.

I got my first real taste of play-by-play doing the games of the Aurora Clippers, a semipro football team.

I supplemented my income by becoming manager of a fast-pitch softball team called the Aurora Foxes.

Ray Gasper

I played on the team, which turned out to be pretty successful. We won our division three times in the late forties, but lost to Ft. Wayne all three times in the fast-pitch World Series.

Chick was a good manager. I remember one time in Rock Island, Illinois, we got into a big argument with the umpire in a game against Quad Cities. Chick told us all to get on the bus and we left.

———

Hearn next moved to WBNU, an FM station in Aurora, where he showed another facet of his announcing ability by hosting a game show called *The Sky's the Limit*, an early version of *Truth or Consequences*, from the top of the Leland Hotel, a skyscraper by Aurora standards. When it was built in 1921, the Leland Hotel, 19 stories high, was the tallest building in Illinois outside of Chicago, according to Dennis Buck, senior curator of the Aurora Historical Society. On the top floor was the Sky Club, from where Hearn did his broadcasts.

Shirley Gruber
Hearn's Sister
I worked as a waitress at the Sky Club, and I remember, when the wind really blew, the water in the glasses would sway.

Chick

There was a state high school basketball tournament known as the Sweet Sixteen held in Champagne-Urbana. When a local school got in, we would send a crew down to broadcast their games. I didn't know if I would ever get the chance to be a part of that but, in my first year at the station, our play-by-play announcer got sick and couldn't make it.

"We are in a bind," the station manager told me. "You can do it. I'll go down with you if you want me to."

He wasn't going to be much help, but off we went. All 16 teams played that first day. I was only supposed to do the Aurora game, but I was having so much fun, I convinced the station to let me do all eight games.

And I would have done more if they had had any more.

———

Hearn did enough to impress Dr. A. J. "Frenchie" Haussler, the vice president of Bradley University in Peoria. Haussler heard Hearn and made him an offer he couldn't afford to pass up: a chance to do play-by-play for Bradley University basketball.

But it was also an offer Hearn couldn't afford to accept. Struggling financially at WBNU, he didn't have the money to move his growing family (a second child, their daughter, Samantha, had been born to the Hearns in 1947) to Peoria. He had to borrow $10,000 from an uncle to make the move.

It was the best move Hearn could have made. Starting in 1950 he did the play-by-play for Bradley University basketball and football and some high school games on WEEK Radio. Later, when WEEK added a television station, Hearn did a nightly sportscast.

The spotlight that had so long eluded Hearn was finally shining on him, but he had to share it. Bradley basketball was so big in Peoria that three local stations carried their games.

While Hearn began to stretch his vocal cords and develop a play-by-play style that would later captivate a city and a sport, there wasn't exactly a dearth of talent flanking him in Bradley's Robertson Memorial Field House.

The other two Peoria play-by-play men were Tom Kelly, who would go on to carve his own niche in L.A. sportscasting, primarily as the voice of the USC Trojans, and Bill King, who would go on to become the voice of the Raiders, in both Oakland and Los Angeles, and the Golden State Warriors.

RALPH LAWLER
L.A. Clipper Broadcaster

WEEK, WIRL, and WMBD were all fighting for the same audience because Bradley basketball was so huge in the fifties. An entire city listened to those games.

It was such a thrill for me growing up in Peoria because, from the time I was in grade school, I was a Bradley fan, and Chick was our broadcaster of choice. We would sit and listen at home. This was not really before TV, but a time when TV wasn't such an important part of your life. Radio still was.

I loved his enthusiasm, his style. I was already dreaming of being a baseball or basketball broadcaster when I grew up. I would tape-record my own play-by-play of games I watched, and my dad would critique them for me. Chick was the inspiration for me in Peoria in the fifties.

I recall specifically running up and down the court as a high school player and hearing his voice say my name. It was an incredible thrill for me because I had heard him broadcasting all those Bradley games. The Bradley players were huge heroes to me, and I had heard him calling their names over the years. And here he was now, calling my name. I just thought it was the coolest thing I had ever heard.

In later years, when I became an NBA announcer and we saw each other all the time, Chick was kind enough to say he remembered me as a player, but I don't believe that. He may have remembered Peoria Central [where Lawler played].

He'd say to me, "You were a good player." Yeah right, Chick, but it was really sweet of him to say that.

TOM KELLY
L.A. Sportscaster

Robertson Memorial Field House at Bradley was quite the place to be in those days. It held about seven thousand to eight thousand fans, and the floor was elevated on sawhorses. It was a hell of a place to play.

You know, they say if it plays in Peoria, it will play anywhere. Chick certainly proved there that he could play anywhere.

Ralph Lawler

My dad, Ralph Sr., had a drive-in theater in Peoria. In those days, you didn't have championship fights on pay-per-view or free local television. They would be shown three days later on film at theaters.

My father would have Chick come out early before his 10 P.M. sportscast and get a private viewing of a major fight in a projection booth. Chick would then hightail it over to East Peoria, where WEEK-TV was, and tell his audience, "I just got done watching the big fight."

Tex Winter
Laker Assistant Now in His 57ᵗʰ Season Coaching in Either Division I College Basketball or Professional Basketball

I was coaching at Marquette, and we went down and played Bradley. I was the youngest major college coach in the nation at that time, just 28.

I a got tape of our game against Bradley on one of those reel-to-reel things because I wanted to review our game. When I heard the tape, I was really impressed with their announcer, Chick Hearn, who was not a whole lot older than I was. I played that tape back several times just to listen to him. It was apparent, even at that time, that he was going to be a big-time announcer. He was very popular at Bradley, a good-looking guy, very dynamic on the radio. Even then, he used a lot of different terms.

Later on, when I got to Kansas State, I recommended him to one of the Kansas City stations as an announcer. I don't know what ever became of that.

———

Thanks to Curt Gowdy, nothing became of it because a Gowdy recommendation helped put Hearn on an even bigger stage.

Curt Gowdy
Named America's Top Sportscaster Seven Times

I did some play-by-play of NBA games for NBC in the fifties. And on two of those games, I worked with a young announcer from Peoria named Chick Hearn.

He really impressed me. That was always my best sport when I was in college at the University of Wyoming, so I felt I knew basketball. It was obvious this guy was good. I was very impressed with him.

So I passed his name along to Tom Gallery, who was then head of NBC Sports. I told him, "Listen, there's a young guy here who is very good, very glib. His name is Chick Hearn, and I think he would be a good guy for you."

Bob Speck
Sports Producer

Jack Buck and Chick were both up for the St. Louis Cardinal baseball play-by-play job. After Buck got it—he, of course, went on to become a legend there—he was also contacted about doing USC football. Not about to do both, Jack recommended Chick for the USC job.

————

Hearn thus found himself presented with a sportscaster's dream: a chance to interview for a radio job on KNX, the CBS affiliate in Los Angeles doing USC football. Except Hearn wasn't so sure it was his dream job. Life was good in Peoria.

Besides, he didn't even have a suit to wear to the interview.

Nevertheless, with his son, Gary, then 14, Hearn hopped a train for Los Angeles, bought a suit on a stopover in Chicago, and landed the job in 1956.

Ralph Lawler

When Chick began the migration to California, it opened a door for some of us to follow him out, starting with Tom Kelly. But when Chick left Peoria, it left a hole in everybody's heart.

~ 3 ~

His Arrival

Coming to Los Angeles to be a sportscaster in 1956 was like going to work for Bill Gates in the late seventies. An explosive period of unimaginable growth and wealth was on the horizon for those discerning enough to see it.

It had been a decade since Cleveland Rams owner Dan Reeves had brought his football team to L.A., lighting the slow-burning fuse of professional sports in Southern California

Until then, California in general, and Los Angeles in particular, had been a golden land of lost opportunities for those who made their living in sports. There was USC football, numerous boxing shows, thriving Pacific Coast League baseball, and winter barnstorming tours by the big leaguers.

But before the advent of jet travel, no owner of a pro club in any sport was about to bear the expense of loading his team on trains or slow-moving aircraft on a regular basis to play games thousands of miles away.

Reeves was the trailblazer but, of course, if any sport was to go west, pro football, with only a single game per week, was the most logical.

So out he came in 1946 with his Cleveland Rams, despite the fact that his team had won the NFL championship the season before and could be expected to profit from increased fan support in Cleveland.

At first it appeared Reeves had made a horrible miscalculation. True, for the Rams' first appearance in their new home, the Los Angeles Coliseum, they drew 68,188 spectators for an exhibition game against the Washington Redskins. But, for the Rams' regular-season opener three weeks later against the Philadelphia Eagles, only 30,553 spectators showed up.

Part of the problem was USC and UCLA loyalists who were turned off by the idea of professional athletes invading their Coliseum turf—long the bastion of the collegiate crowd. The line between professional and amateur sports was more clearly drawn in those days. And the Coliseum was considered a haven for amateurs, from those in the 1932 Olympics to the Trojans and Bruins.

Another factor was the arrival, along with Reeves, of a competitor. The All-America Football Conference began play in 1946 with one of its entries being the Los Angeles Dons. And they too laid claim to an increasingly congested Coliseum.

But if the Dons were indeed stealing fans from the Rams, they weren't stealing many. The Dons averaged around ten thousand spectators for their first three home games.

Such lukewarm reaction to the arrival of the pros caused local columnists to agonize in print over the thought that L.A. was blowing its long-awaited moment to join its eastern brethren as a hot spot for the pros.

In a letter to the *Los Angeles Times*, dated November 10, 1946, a fan named Aldo Molinari wrote:

> The Rams and Dons are splendid, but this is only their first year.
> If they continue good football, the fans soon will appear.
> Time is a great healer, we've oft heard it cracked.
> Give the pros sufficient time and the Coliseum will be packed.

It took a while, but Molinari was correct.

At least for the Rams.

The Dons disappeared after the 1949 season, as did their young conference, when the NFL absorbed three AAFC franchises: the Baltimore Colts, the San Francisco 49ers, and the Cleveland Browns.

But the Rams proved Reeves' judgment had been sound. By 1949 they were averaging 51,555 fans per game. Winning the NFL title in 1951 further enhanced their popularity. The Rams went on to draw more than one hundred thousand spectators three times and more than eighty thousand spectators thirty times before leaving L.A. in 1979 for Anaheim.

Such overwhelming support soon drew the interest of other owners in other sports who saw what was going on in the hinterlands of L.A. with raised eyebrows and visions of dollars signs dancing in their collective heads.

But in 1956, when the Hearns—Chick, Marge, 14-year-old Gary, and 9-year-old Samantha—arrived in L.A. in their bright red Chevrolet, Walter O'Malley was still dreaming of a domed stadium for his Brooklyn Dodgers, Bob Short was still dreaming of buying the once-dominant Minneapolis Lakers, and Jack Kent Cooke was still dreaming of bringing the National Hockey League to a land where ice was most likely to be found at the bottom of a glass.

All those dreams were about to be realized.

As were those of Chick Hearn.

Any doubts that the farm boy from the Midwest could relate to a star-struck city weaned on glamour and garishness were soon quelled. Hearn, with his wit, his sarcasm, and his showmanship, was perfect for a populace easily tempted and quickly bored.

Hearn knew sports, and he knew how to deliver it in an appealing manner to an audience always spinning the radio dial in search of new attractions. They kept their dial tuned to Hearn after they discovered him doing USC football and basketball.

And NBC, remembering the recommendation of Curt Gowdy, soon discovered Hearn as well. In addition to doing USC and nightly sportscasts on KNX, Hearn became the nightly sportscaster on Channel 4, the NBC affiliate in L.A., before Ross Porter, before Stu Nahan, before Fred Roggin.

———

On January 18, 1960, a DC-3 carrying the Minneapolis Lakers through a hellacious snowstorm crash-landed in a cornfield in Carroll, Iowa. It was hours before the outside world realized there was a problem, a problem that, fortunately, did not result in any injuries.

29

The lack of attention the crash garnered further illustrated that it wasn't just the skies of Iowa that had suffered from a visibility problem. The Lakers had won five NBA titles in Minneapolis. They were also the champions of the National Basketball League during the 1947–1948 season. They had George Mikan, the NBA's first superstar, and fellow future Hall of Famers Slater Martin, Vern Mikkelsen, Jim Pollard, Clyde Lovellette, and coach John Kundla.

Yet they didn't have a fan base. Sometimes, as few as a thousand paying customers would show up for games.

Bob Short, a Minneapolis businessman who had made his fortune in the trucking and hotel businesses, was so anxious to keep the club in Minneapolis that he joined 19 others in putting up $150,000 to purchase the Lakers in 1957.

But that, as Short soon learned, was just the beginning.

His group came up with another $50,000 for operating expenses. That lasted two weeks. At one point, the club desperately needed $14,000 just to stay afloat. Short wrote out a check for that amount and, in exchange, was handed all of the team's outstanding common stock, worth five cents a share. That gave Short a full third of the club.

But he could clearly see that a third of nothing was still nothing.

And he could also see what was going on in Los Angeles, where O'Malley, having given up on the idea of getting a stadium deal in Brooklyn, had moved his Dodgers in 1958.

Unlike the Rams, who became an acquired taste in L.A., the Dodgers were an immediate feast for fans who had previously supported the Los Angeles Angels and Hollywood Stars of the Pacific Coast League.

A total of 78,672 spectators poured into the Coliseum for the Dodgers' first home opener, and they kept coming. More than 93,000 people attended an exhibition game against the New York Yankees on Roy Campanella Night in 1959. More than 92,000 attended each of the three World Series games played against the Chicago White Sox that season in the Coliseum.

And then there was Short, stuck in Minneapolis, trying to figure out where the next team meal was coming from.

He decided to move the Lakers to L.A. after the 1959–1960 season. There was no expectation that they'd come close to equaling the Rams or the

Dodgers in popularity. After all, the NBA was still a bush league compared to the NFL and major league baseball. And, with UCLA still four years away from the start of the John Wooden dynasty, college basketball hadn't exactly electrified the town.

Both UCLA and USC played their home games in the new Sports Arena, better known as the building where the Democrats nominated John F. Kennedy as their presidential candidate in 1960.

Now it was Short who was envisioning a journey to a new frontier, where he would join the Bruins and Trojans as Sports Arena tenants.

Still, before he made the final commitment, Short wanted to test these uncharted waters. So he scheduled regular-season games against the Philadelphia Warriors for January 30, 1960, in San Francisco, and on February 1 at the Sports Arena. There was also to be a prelim game at the Sports Arena that night between the Los Alamitos navy squad and the Vagabonds, a group who billed themselves as "an all-Negro basketball team."

The historic West Coast swing was scheduled for just 11 days after that Laker trip had ended prematurely in that cornfield. Some players weren't too happy about spending even more time in the air. Especially in a DC-3. And there was plenty of grumbling from their wives as well.

But Short explained the financial facts of life, and the Lakers acquiesced.

The Warriors beat the Lakers 103–96 in that first L.A. appearance, but Short wasn't unhappy because the game drew 10,202 spectators.

"We don't want to leave Minneapolis," he told the L.A. media on that trip, "[but] if we can't see a way to operate without constantly subsidizing our investment, we'd ask permission to move our franchise."

The Lakers played two more test games at the Sports Arena that season and drew a total of 8,300 fans.

Still, it was better than Short could expect in Minneapolis. And, with the crowd-pleasing skills of Elgin Baylor and the prospect of drafting an exciting young kid from West Virginia named Jerry West for the following season, the Lakers figured to be an attractive draw in a new town.

Short would make the move. All he needed was league approval.

But he couldn't get it. Fellow owners, not wishing to incur additional travel expenses, voted 7–1 against the move, the one being Short.

He predicted the Lakers would die in Minneapolis. All he got back from the other owners was shrugs.

But one person the NBA owners couldn't shrug off was Abe Saperstein. The man behind the highly successful Harlem Globetrotters, Saperstein announced the formation of a rival basketball organization, the American Basketball League, just about the time the NBA was ordering wreaths for the Lakers.

Suddenly, Los Angeles had become coveted territory. Surely if the Lakers didn't move to L.A., Saperstein would claim the territory as his own

The NBA voted again on the Laker move. This time, the vote was 8–0. In favor. Short could roll the dice on his gamble.

"A gamble?" he later said. "Hell, we were broke in Minneapolis."

The Lakers didn't exactly rake in the profits upon their arrival in Los Angeles either. Despite the addition of West and a 34.8 scoring average by Baylor, the Lakers' average attendance during their first season in L.A. was only 5,045.

They had such little pull that they couldn't even get the Sports Arena for all their home games. One had to be played at California State at Los Angeles, another at the Shrine Auditorium.

Although they finished 36–43, the Lakers qualified for the playoffs—the standards obviously weren't very high—and beat the Detroit Pistons 3–2 in the best-of-five opening round.

Ahead lay the powerful St. Louis Hawks, who had reached the NBA Finals the season before, only to lose to Boston.

It was an exciting time for the Lakers. Too bad nobody seemed to notice. Game 1 of the Piston series at the Sports Arena drew 3,549 fans. It wasn't much better for Game 2, with only 4,253 paying their way in. For the fifth and decisive game, which was played at the Shrine Auditorium, the attendance was 3,705.

Not much changed for the Hawk series. The first two games were played at Cal State Los Angeles, where the seating was limited.

Short needed to sell this series. He needed to sell his team. He needed a spark. He needed to put the games on radio, as much as he hated to pay for it. Without a broadcast outlet, he was dead.

And finally, with a deal to air the remaining games on KNX, Short needed a charismatic announcer. He needed Chick Hearn.

CHICK

The Lakers were bringing in about four thousand people a game. I get a call at home at about 2:00 in the morning. It's Bob Short, owner of the Lakers. He wants to know if, as part of his new radio deal, I would fly out to St. Louis to do the game.

———

Short got a deal, Hearn got a flight, and the Lakers got a play-by-play announcer for the ages. His first broadcast came on March 27, 1961, with the Lakers beating the Hawks 121–112 to take a 3–2 lead in the best-of-seven series.

When the Lakers returned to the Sports Arena for Game 6, 14,844 fans showed up, nearly double the *two* Sports Arena crowds in the first round against Detroit. Was it the team's success that had drawn them? They'd been having success all along. No—more than likely, it was the announcer.

The Lakers lost that game and the series, but they didn't lose their play-by-play man. Not for 42 years.

Still, although he became the Laker announcer, Hearn wasn't about to give up his other jobs.

STU NAHAN
L.A. Sportscaster Who Later Became the Channel 4 Sports Anchor

Chick wanted to do both the Lakers and the NBC nightly sportscasts. So he set up a deal where this helicopter would pick him up at the Sports Arena and fly him over to Channel 4 in Burbank in time to do sports on the 11:00 news.

He didn't even have time to write the sportscast, but I remember he would sit on the edge of his desk on the set and ad-lib it. This is how he did it.

I was working for the NBC station in Sacramento. We would get a feed from Channel 4 in Los Angeles, and I would wonder, how does he do that? How can he do a whole sportscast without even writing a couple of words to guide him?

But he did it.

Marge Hearn

Fran and I would drive to the Laker games, and then the helicopter would take him over to Channel 4. I would drive the car over to their Burbank studio, wait for him, and then we would drive home.

———

Helicopters weren't Hearn's only mode of travel. He once hopped on the back of a motorcycle following a USC football game to get from the Coliseum to the airport to catch a flight to a Laker away game.

Such effort may have been applauded in most circles, but not in the office of USC Athletic Director Jess Hill.

Tom Kelly
L.A. Sportscaster

Jess Hill would not allow Chick to continue doing USC football and basketball if he was going to do the Lakers. It was an antiquated feeling, but he decided USC was going to have to get another announcer.

He allowed Chick to do both in 1961, but after that, Chick was going to have to make a choice.

———

For Chick, there was no choice. The Lakers had become his life.

~ 4 ~

His Word's-Eye View

One team came from the land of a thousand lakes, the other from a borough of trolley dodgers. And in 1965, they nearly came together in what would have been the biggest sports merger in Southern California history.

Call it Dodgers-Lakers. Or call it "Dakers" for short. Whatever the name, the new entity would have totally altered the sports landscape forever if Bob Short had agreed to merge his Lakers with Walter O'Malley's Dodgers.

Under the plan, O'Malley would own 80 percent of the combined operation, Bob Short and his attorney, Frank Ryan, the other 20 percent. And the Lakers would have a new facility, to be built in Chavez Ravine adjacent to Dodger Stadium.

But negotiations for the blockbuster deal stalled while O'Malley devoted his attention to a television deal for his baseball team. And during that period of limbo, a multimillionaire named Jack Kent Cooke stepped in and started waving huge sums of money at Short, a man easily tempted by the green.

Cooke, born and raised in Canada, was a skilled and tough negotiator who refused to be denied, a trait he learned while selling encyclopedias door-to-door as an 18-year-old during the Great Depression. He graduated from that to become a soap salesman.

By the age of 24 Cooke had joined a publishing and broadcasting company, where he earned $25 a week. Within 18 months he owned one-third of another communications company.

Eventually expanding his business interests into the United States, Cooke became fixated on owning a sports franchise. He went after an American

League expansion team for Los Angeles, a team to be called the Angels, but lost out to a group led by Gene Autry.

By 1965 Cooke was being advised that the Lakers, always short on dollars with Bob Short but long on potential, would be an attractive purchase.

Cooke had never seen a professional basketball game. Nevertheless, with the Boston Celtics having been sold around that time for $3 million, Cooke offered Short $5 million. Short called O'Malley, who told him he'd be crazy to turn down that kind of money.

So the Dakers never came into existence.

But before Short signed on the dotted line, he decided to squeeze a little more money out of Cooke. He informed Cooke that because he had already sold $350,000 worth of season tickets, he wanted half of that money.

The price was now $5,175,000.

Cooke, having come so close to getting a team, wasn't about to lose out again. He grudgingly paid the additional $175,000.

With Cooke's arrival, Chick Hearn's role with the Lakers expanded. Cooke, a demanding perfectionist, felt a kinship with Hearn, who was himself a perfectionist when it came to the Lakers.

Cooke and Hearn had another thing in common: they were both master showmen.

And while Cooke would never admit it, he knew nothing about basketball. So he promoted Hearn to assistant general manager and leaned on him often for advice in running the club.

But it was clear from the start that this was no partnership. Jack Kent Cooke didn't grant equal status to anyone in his far-flung business empire. Hearn, like everybody else in the organization, was expected to defer to the man at the top and refer to him in respectful tones as Mr. Cooke.

Cooke periodically came down hard on Hearn, as he did on all his employees.

CHICK

The Lakers played a neutral-court game in Long Beach against the old Cincinnati Royals—Oscar Robertson and that group.

The next morning at 6:30 I got a call from Mr. Cooke's secretary, Rosemary Garmand, who said Mr. Cooke wanted to see me.

We were leaving on a road trip that day, but when Mr. Cooke wanted to see you, you'd better be there. So I went down to his office at the Forum.

When I walked in, he said, in that strict tone that commanded attention, "Sit down, Mr. Hearn."

He had some tapes in front of him, and he put one on a machine. Then he took out a big, yellow stenographer's pad, about 18 inches long.

I had no idea what he was doing, but I was scared to death.

Mr. Cooke turned on the machine—the tape turned out to be from the previous night's game—and started to listen, his head cocked and his eyes narrowed.

Every now and then, he'd make a mark on that yellow pad. There was no conversation between us.

At the end of the play-by-play of the first quarter, Mr. Cooke shut off the machine. He looked at his pad, paused in that dramatic way of his, and then, speaking in his smooth, deliberate manner, told me, "You said 15 times—15, Mr. Hearn—how great Cincinnati was. Twice, you mentioned that the Lakers played well."

I nodded and said, "That's right."

"How do you account for that?" he asked.

"What was the score at the end of the quarter?" I replied.

"I don't know what the score was," he said impatiently.

"Well," I said, "I'll tell you. The score was 43–10 in favor of Cincinnati. Do you want me to make a fool of myself? And of you?"

"No," he said. "Get out of here and go on your trip."

———

Not even Jack Kent Cooke was going to sway Hearn from the impartiality he felt was crucial to a broadcast.

STU NAHAN
L.A. Sportscaster Who Later Became the Channel 4 Sports Anchor

When you are a play-by-play broadcaster doing a particular team's games, you are not supposed to be a homer. Chick wanted the Lakers to win. He would sometimes say something like, "Well, we've got to get four points here to win the game."

But he wasn't like Harry Caray in Chicago. Chick would give credit to the other team if they did something well. He would always do that.

And he would knock the Lakers when he felt they deserved it: "How come there was no defender there? Doesn't anybody box out for the rebound?"

He was someone for the rest of us to look up to, someone you would want to guide your career.

———

When Jerry Buss bought the team from Cooke in 1979, he didn't try to change his legendary announcer.

JERRY BUSS
Laker Owner

Chick was not a homer.

He really took a lot of pride in calling it exactly as he saw it without softening it for the home crowd. That infuriated some people.

On the other hand, over the years, you began to appreciate it because you knew what he was calling was what was actually happening.

———

Hearn's insistence on impartiality was hardly foreign to L.A. It was also strictly adhered to by the city's other legendary figure behind the mike.

VIN SCULLY
Dodger Broadcaster

I came from New York. We had three teams, and I remember Red Barber [the man who broke Scully in] tried very hard to go down the middle. So that's the way I was brought up in the business. With me, it was what I inherited, and I knew I had better toe the line.

And then, coming out to Los Angeles, I remember Mr. O'Malley said to me, "You know, we're all alone out here. Maybe you ought to start to root."

And I said to him, "Mr. O'Malley, I wouldn't know how. After eight years of trying so hard to play it down the middle, I hope I don't have to change."

And he said, "OK, that's good enough for me." And that's what we did.

———

While Cooke would grudgingly allow Hearn his impartiality, it wasn't an allowance Cooke extended to his other play-by-play man.

BOB MILLER
L.A. Kings Broadcaster

Chick was put in charge of finding a hockey announcer for the Kings, which I know he didn't really want to have to do. It was 1972, and I was in Madison, Wisconsin, doing University of Wisconsin hockey, basketball, and football. I heard the Kings had an opening and Chick was in charge of the search, so I sent him a tape and resume.

He called me and said, "I really like your tape, and I'm going to suggest to Mr. Cooke that you get the job."

Months went on and I never heard anything back. Finally, at a convention in Chicago, I asked somebody from L.A. if the Kings had ever gotten an announcer, and I was told that they had hired someone just the week before. It was Roy Storey.

This was during the period when Chick's son, Gary, had died. Chick had left town, but had left word to hire me. Instead, Mr. Cooke hired Storey.

The next season, I sent Chick some updated material just in case anything happened, because I had heard the Kings weren't too happy with their announcing situation. Chick called me, told me to come out, and I wound up signing a contract.

While I was out in L.A., I wanted to listen to Chick do a game. I wanted to hear his style. The night I was listening, he was just ripping the Lakers. He was saying things like, "Happy Hairston leads the world in blown layups," and, "This is the worst I've ever seen a team play."

So I thought, well, I guess that's what they want.

The next night, I did a Kings game. At one point, there was a two-on-one break for the Kings, and the player didn't even get a shot. So I said, "He should have shot. I don't know what he's passing for."

The next day, Mr. Cooke called me into the office and told me, "I don't ever want to hear you second-guessing those players. It's a lot easier from where you're sitting than it is on the ice."

I was thinking, there's a double standard here. I just heard a guy last night really ripping players. But I found out in a hurry from Mr. Cooke that's not what he wanted from me.

———

Impartiality was unheard of in some cities, where homers were not only tolerated, but encouraged. Nevertheless, Hearn was never condescending about rival announcers.

BOB KEISSER
Long Beach Press-Telegram Media Critic

Whenever people in my business would criticize [Celtic announcers] Johnny Most and Tommy Heinsohn, Chick would defend them vociferously.

He would say, "Boston is not L.A. It's a different market. Critics here are different. If you have ever been in Boston, you know how important Johnny Most is to the community, and you know what Tommy Heinsohn means to them."

Chick took the high road whenever he could.

———————

While Hearn may not have publicly rooted for the Lakers, his loyalty sometimes came through anyway.

Scott Ostler
Former Laker Beat Writer for the *Los Angeles Times*

Chick had a stock phrase when things were going badly and the offense was stagnant. He'd scream into the microphone: "The Lakers are standing around! The Lakers are standing around!"

I came to realize he never said that about the other team. He never screamed, "The Pistons are standing around!" Because he didn't care about the other team. He cared about the Lakers.

When you take your kids to a party and all the kids there are being bad, you don't care about the other kids. You care that your kid is being bad.

The Lakers were like his kids.

Roy Firestone
National Sportscaster Who also Did a Laker Pregame Show from 1985–1991

Chick treated the players like his sons. Let them screw up, and he would be horrified, angry, and would chastise them on the air. He could show such disdain, saying things like, "Byron Scott takes a shot *needlessly.*"

There was a conflicting image there. On the one hand, Chick could be cheerful, playful, an almost mascot-like announcer for the Lakers. But he could also be cantankerous, very cranky.

STEVE HARTMAN
L.A. Sportscaster and Talk-Show Host

Chick was never inhibited in terms of being critical of the Lakers if he thought they deserved it.

Back when Chet [Forte] and I were doing our radio talk show together, we brought on Chick during a time when the Lakers were in a down period.

It was early in the career of Vlade [Divac], and he was struggling. We asked Chick about Vlade, and he said, "He is so terrible, they ought to send him back to wherever he came from. He can't play the game."

I have never, ever heard him be that critical of a player. But he could be tough and that's what we loved about him.

PAT WILLIAMS
Orlando Magic Executive

Chick always did the interviewing, and was rarely interviewed. But having had him on my talk show, I want to tell you, he was a fabulous interview because he could not dance around the truth for all the money in the world. He was constitutionally incapable of doing anything but sharing exactly what he felt.

You'd ask him, "How is Shaq doing?"

He'd say, "Shaq is playing very poorly."

You'd ask him, "How are Shaq and Kobe getting along?"

He'd say, "Not well at all, Pat."

That was Chick.

JIM HILL
L.A. Sportscaster

One night Chick was down on the floor at halftime receiving one of the many tributes he got over the years from the Lakers. But on this particular night, the Lakers were playing very poorly.

Chick, microphone in hand, was saying all the right things, thanking everybody. But then he added, "Now let's get to the second half. Hopefully, the Lakers will play better than they did in the first half, because in the first half, they played like a bunch of dogs."

———

Hearn would agonize over the Laker fortunes. For him, the slightest problem was a snowball gathering speed.

MITCH CHORTKOFF
Former Laker Beat Writer for the *Santa Monica Outlook*

We were on the Laker bus, and the team had just lost their second exhibition game. It meant nothing because the coaches were experimenting with different players. Nobody could take the Laker record seriously under those circumstances.

Chick tapped me on the shoulder, looked around to see if anybody was listening, pulled me close, and said quietly, "The goal of this team now should be no more than to just make the playoffs."

It went on to become one of their championship seasons.

———

Hearn once began a broadcast by telling his audience that the struggling Lakers were faced with their biggest game of the year.

The team was indeed struggling. It was 1–2 in the regular season with only 79 games to go.

Impartiality wasn't the only issue when Cooke sent for Hearn.

BOB MILLER

When I was in my first year with the Kings, Jack Kent Cooke called Chick and me into his office. Mr. Cooke had come up with some of the craziest things, and he wanted us to do them on the air. And Chick was agreeing with him.

Mr. Cooke said to me, "Get the sponsors into the broadcast more. Say, 'There's Marcel Dionne scooting down the ice like a Datsun.'"

"Wonderful idea, Mr. Cooke," Chick said.

I was thinking, "Chick, what are you agreeing to? That's the worst suggestion I've ever heard."

Then Mr. Cooke came up with something else off the wall, and Chick again told him what a wonderful idea it was.

When we left Mr. Cooke's office and were walking down the hall, Chick told me, "That silly son of a gun. We're not doing any of that stuff."

"Maybe you aren't," I said, "but I'm in my first year. What you've just agreed to, I'm going to have to do."

———

Hearn and Cooke. Everybody seems to have a story about them.

BILL SHARMAN
Laker Coach and Front-Office Executive

After Jack Kent Cooke had sold the Lakers, he asked Chick to do one of the exhibition games for his football team, the Washington Redskins.

When the game was over, Cooke told him, "Chick, you did a wonderful job. By the way, how much are the Lakers paying you?"

Chick gave him a figure.

"Oh my gosh," Cooke said, "you are worth a lot more than that."

"Yeah," Chick agreed, "that's what I thought when you signed me to this Laker contract three years ago."

BOB MILLER

Some nights a telecast really goes well, and everything clicks. You are good as an announcer, and everybody is on the same page. Chick told me that the Lakers had one of those telecasts in Milwaukee one season, one of their best in a long time.

The next day, Mr. Cooke called Chick in Kansas City, where the Lakers had gone for their next game, and asked, "Chick, what was wrong with you last night?"

Chick told me he couldn't believe what he was hearing. "What do you mean?" he asked Mr. Cooke.

"Well, you weren't very good," Mr. Cooke said. "I had friends over to watch the game, and they all said the same thing: what's wrong with Chick?"

Chick told me he was furious because he knew they had done an almost perfect telecast. "Mr. Cooke," Chick told him, "we'll be home tomorrow. You get those friends, and I'll buy them lunch at the Forum Club, and I want them to tell me that to my face."

"Chick," Cooke replied, "I couldn't embarrass my friends like that."

If you were in the organization, whether you were a coach or a player or a broadcaster, and Mr. Cooke thought you were getting too big for your britches, he would knock you down a few pegs. And I think that's what Chick thought he was doing.

CLAIRE ROTHMAN
Former Executive Under Both Jack Kent Cooke and Jerry Buss

Jack Kent Cooke hired a young director, Marty Ehrlick, whose work he had admired on Boston Celtic telecasts. Mr. Cooke gave Marty very definite instructions about what he wanted to see on Laker telecasts. My assistant, Gene Felling, was to handle the details and make sure Mr. Cooke's instructions were followed.

One night on the first long road trip after the pecking order had been established, Mr. Cooke was at the Forum, where a rock concert was going on, but he was on the phone with Gene, ranting about the camera movement in a game being played on the East Coast. He wanted it stopped. Period.

In the midst of his verbal blast, Mr. Cooke didn't take into consideration the time difference. What he was watching was a delayed broadcast. In reality, the game was over and no changes could be made.

Mr. Cooke threatened Gene, telling him that, if corrections were not made, he would be banished from his job.

Hearing this, I was upset for Gene and concerned about losing this very competent assistant.

Fortunately, Chick heard from Mr. Cooke as well and reminded him of the time difference. Nothing could be done, he told Mr. Cooke. Not on that broadcast.

Chick followed up for the remainder of the trip with phone calls. How was Gene? Had Mr. Cooke's tirades ceased?

Such a loyal friend, Chick called to offer me encouragement every day of that trip.

———

In 1975, in one of many letters Cooke wrote to Hearn, Cooke said, "You know what I think of you. In short, I think you're one of the finest men I have had the great fortune to know in my life."

———

Over the years, there were so many terms used by Hearn on the air—so original, yet so different from one another, they could only be described with one word: Chickisms. They were tools Hearn used to describe what he saw on the court—his own personal vocabulary. Today, those terms have been used so often by other announcers, and even incorporated into everyday language to such an extent that many fail to remember where they came from.

Seal a business deal with ease. Pass a classroom test without missing an answer. Win an election in a landslide. All of those efforts might elicit the same response: it was a slam dunk.

But how many people know that Hearn invented that term? He also invented:

Chick was born
Francis Dayle Hearn
in Buda, Illinois.

Chick, at age six or
seven, models his
school baseball
uniform.

An accomplished softball player, Chick makes the stretch at first base.

Chick (back row, second from left) poses with the members of his AAU basketball team, the very fellows who nicknamed him "Chick."

Chick and Marge were high school sweethearts and married three years after graduation, in 1938.

Chick's first big broadcasting break came from WEEK in Peoria, Illinois, for which he did radio and some television and blossomed into something of a local celebrity.

Upon taking a job to broadcast USC football games, Chick loaded up the family in 1956 for the big move from Peoria to Los Angeles.

Chick and daughter Samantha in 1960.

The Hearn family foursome: Samantha, Chick, Marge, and Gary.

Marge and Chick—by this time a big name in Los Angeles—no doubt on the banquet circuit.

Son Gary at age 18.

Gary's daughter, Shannon Hearn-Newman, with Chick and Marge's great-granddaughter, Kayla.

Samantha at the height of her modeling career.

- no harm, no foul
- faked him into the popcorn machine
- the mustard's off the hot dog
- air ball
- it'll count if it goes
- he did the bunny hop in the pea patch
- dribble drive
- didn't draw iron
- ticky-tack foul
- word's-eye view

And of course, the classic: this game's in the refrigerator, the door's closed, the light's out, the eggs are cooling, the butter's getting hard, and the Jell-O's jiggling.

JAMES WORTHY
Former Laker

When we used to play the Hornets in Charlotte, my mother, Gladys, who lived there, would cook for the whole team. Chick loved her sweet potato pie, so she started cooking a special one for him, and they became good friends.

She'd stay up and listen to him late at night on the satellite. At that point, he'd talk about the game being in the refrigerator, but he didn't have the whole thing. It was my mother who told him, "Why don't you finish it up by saying the eggs are cooling and the Jell-O's jiggling?"

So Chick gave me my nickname—Big Game James—and my mother gave him that Chickism.

PAUL SUNDERLAND
Hearn's Successor

Everybody talks about his famous lexicon, thinking that he sat home at night trying to think up clever things. I think I'm right in saying that it all developed naturally in the flow of the game and the flow of the life around the game over four decades. That's how it came to be.

Tom Kelly
L.A. Sportscaster

I've known a lot of truly great basketball announcers, but I don't know anybody who had the terminology that Hearn did over the years. Everybody uses them now, but they are Hearnisms. He started them.

He became as good as any basketball announcer who ever lived. From baseline to baseline, nobody did basketball better. He was every bit the best.

Bill Macdonald
L.A. Sportscaster

He has remained so influential for all of us, affecting my style, everybody's style. Chickisms: we all use them on occasion. You can't help it.

Jaime Jarrin
Dodger Spanish-Language Broadcaster

It is a very unique experience. In my case, I had to teach the game of baseball to the audience because Latin American fans coming from South America and Central America didn't know a lot about baseball, or they didn't care much about baseball.

I had to teach them what it meant to say a batter was out 4–3 [second to first] or 6–3 [short to first], or what a fly out to 8 [center field] was. I had to start with the basic idea that each player has a number based on his defensive position, not the number on the back of his uniform.

Chick, in a way, did the same thing. He introduced so many idioms, so many special words. It was just amazing the way he did that.

Vin Scully

Chick Hearn was the bridge from the ballclub to the fan. He was an expert, and you knew he was an expert, but he never really tried to sound like an expert.

The biggest thing of all about Chick, as far as I'm concerned, was that he was so human. People related to him instantaneously.

He was so valuable to the Lakers. He was as much a part of the team as any of the players who ever played.

JERRY BUSS

He was totally unique. There was another guy I really liked to listen to, Johnny Most with the Boston Celtics. Those were the two characters of all time. It was interesting that one was with the Lakers and one was with the Celtics, that these two great rivals had these legendary announcers.

I learned about professional basketball through Chick. Even when I had season tickets before I owned the team, when the Lakers were on the road, I used to listen to Chick.

He would say things like, "You need a timeout here." And coming out of a timeout, "You gotta score." He made you think and taught you about the game.

ROY FIRESTONE

In Chick's prime, no man ever had a greater syncopation, a feel for the pace of a game. He had rhythm, cadence, and a desire to be equal to the greatness of the game. Nobody else ever had such a feel to that extent. Not Vin Scully nor Red Barber, two men I consider worthy of being on Mt. Rushmore. Chick may have exceeded them. He was the voice of his game. You have to have an ego to feel as big as the game, and Chick had that. But he needed it.

He had the ability to make every minute of a game sound like the biggest thing in the world. That's the sign of a great announcer. And a great showman. To say he sold tickets is the greatest understatement of all.

He could work anything into the broadcast. I remember this esteemed doctor in the community had died, and Chick said, "Hearts are heavy tonight. We have lost a great physician. Magic makes the free throw." Offered his condolence, but didn't miss a second of the game.

In the four seconds it might take for a player to move to the basket, Chick would come up with a line that was so funny, so witty, it was probably better than anything he could have come up with if he had had four months to think about it. Throwaway lines would just roll out of his mouth.

When he first became an announcer back in the Midwest, he learned to fly by the seat of his pants. Those guys back in those days got no help.

Chick was first and foremost a radio announcer. He became a radio announcer who did television, but he never stopped being a radio announcer.

The fact that Chick Hearn was not on network television for the NBA Finals was a crime. The nation missed a lot by not getting to hear him.

With all the greatness of the Lakers over the years, he was the biggest Laker of them all.

BILL MACDONALD

What made Chick so unique was the fact that he could blend so many things into each broadcast. He could be witty, he could be funny, he could be sarcastic, he could be informative, and he could be entertaining.

One of the things I enjoyed so much about his broadcasts was that they were never forced. I've listened to guys who talked fast. Chick talked fast, but he didn't talk fast, if you know what I mean. His cadence of delivery was perfect.

ALAN MASSENGALE
L.A. Sportscaster

On the 25th anniversary of Laker broadcasts on Channel 9, Chick came in to our studio to go through every year.

And he remembered every year.

I would just give him a season and a circumstance, and he went straight through it. And he was prodding me the whole time, saying, "Come on, let's move faster. Let's get this done. Come on, you can do this."

If I got a name wrong or something else wrong about the year, he'd catch it immediately and let me know.

He was being his professional, cantankerous self.

I was amazed. At my age, about half his, I can't remember what I did last week, but he remembered all situations, everything, over 25 years.

———

Whatever the situation, Hearn always seemed to come up with the perfect line.

JIM HILL

It's 1979. The Lakers have a coin toss with the Chicago Bulls to determine who is going to get the first pick in the upcoming draft. It's an especially big deal because it's the year Magic Johnson is coming out. The Bulls and the then–New Orleans Jazz got the top two picks by finishing last in their conferences. But the Lakers had previously gotten the Jazz pick through a trade.

I'm in a room at the Forum with Bill Sharman, who was then the Laker general manager, and Chick, who was then the assistant general manager. NBA Commissioner Larry O'Brien, Laker officials in L.A., and Bull officials in Chicago are all hooked up on a conference call.

Rod Thorn, who was the Chicago general manager at the time, was to make the call on a coin that is being flipped in New York.

He calls heads. It comes up tails.

There's this roar in the Forum office, led by Chick.

And then, as only Chick could do it, he says, "That's the first thing we've won in a week."

PAUL SUNDERLAND

There was this great Laker game that went into overtime and then double overtime. At every timeout, they went to a commercial, and Chick was getting really sick of it.

Finally, with a few seconds left, and the Lakers on the verge of winning, Chick said on the air, "We're going to take another commercial break on the very *expensive* Fox Sports Network."

———

It's not just the talent and the one-liners that sportscasters remember when they think of Hearn. It's also the personal touch.

BILL MACDONALD

I can still vividly remember the end of that third game of the 1970 NBA Finals between the Lakers and the Knicks. Just a kid, I was supposed to be asleep by then. Instead, I had the radio on in my room. By the time Jerry West took that shot from beyond midcourt to tie the game, with Chick describing it, I was on the edge of my bed. I never forget that.

I first met Chick when I was working out of the Forum, doing P.R. and Lazers indoor soccer. I was so nervous the first time I encountered him. After all, this guy had been one of my heroes. I couldn't believe how nice Chick was to me. And he was always that same way, always gracious, always encouraging.

His last two or three years, every single game I was at Staples Center, I would go up and say hi to him, right up until his last days on the air. It meant so much to me, thrilled me, that Chick knew me and always had a smile for me. I never lost that thrill over his reaction to seeing me.

When I did my first indoor soccer game, I sat in Chick's nest, high above the western sidelines. As I was about to go on the air, I thought, "If I'm in Chick's seat, I've made it."

JOHN IRELAND
L.A. Sportscaster

When Chick was about to do his 3,000th straight Laker game, I and other television reporters went down to the Forum to reminisce with him about his fondest memories. To make it easy on everybody, Laker P.R. director John Black set up a two-hour block in which each of us would have 20 minutes to sit down with Chick. Each station set up at a different spot on the court.

When he finished with the station ahead of me, Chick walked over to where I was set up and asked, "Are you ready to go?"

He then opened the briefcase he was holding and I saw he had seven ties in there.

"I don't want to look the same on every channel," he said, "so I brought seven different ones."

I thought that was so cool.

ALAN MASSENGALE

Working in Miami, I'm leaving a game in which the Lakers have just destroyed the Miami Heat. It was the first year of the Heat's existence.

I get to my car—I had a little Corvette two-seater—and I'm just getting ready to leave when this guy comes out of the shadows and says, "Hey, young man, could I have a ride?"

I look up and, my God, it's Chick Hearn. I've never met him.

"I missed my bus," he says. "I need a ride back to the hotel. You going my way?"

"Sure," I say, "get in."

He doesn't know that I know he's a legend, and he doesn't know he's a legend, doesn't know he's Chick Hearn. Vin Scully doesn't just come out and get in your car, OK?

Chick crams himself into this little Corvette, and I'm riding down the road thinking, "This is unreal. I've got one of the most famous sports announcers in the country sitting in my car."

I don't even remember what I talked to him about, but it was like he was my best friend.

~ 5 ~
His Streak

3,338 Straight Games: November 21, 1965–December 16, 2001

Jack Kent Cooke knew he had the best basketball announcer on the planet, and he didn't want to share him.

In 1965 Chick Hearn missed a Laker game to do a golf tournament for NBC. It would to be the first and last time over a 42-year span that he would miss a game by choice.

It didn't take much urging by Cooke for Hearn to agree after that to always make the Lakers his top priority. Hearn loved to stay busy, loved to keep a broadcasting schedule that would exhaust the fittest of athletes. But there was nothing Hearn enjoyed as much as sitting at a microphone with his Lakers running up and down the court in front of him.

Still, Hearn wasn't about to totally give up his outside assignments. And that left Cooke fearful that, with a schedule that ran through the dead of winter and an airline system far less flexible in the sixties than it is today, Hearn would get stuck somewhere, unable to make it back in time for a Laker tipoff. So Cooke chartered private jets to whisk Hearn from his outside work to the site of his team's next game.

Nevertheless, on a bitter winter night, November 20, 1965, Cooke's nightmare became Hearn's reality. After broadcasting a football game between the University of Arkansas and Texas Tech in Fayetteville, Arkansas, Hearn had a private plane waiting to take him to Las Vegas, where the Lakers were to play the San Francisco Warriors that night.

Instead, Hearn decided to stay on the ground in Fayetteville upon the advice of his pilot.

ROY FIRESTONE
National Sportscaster Who also Did a Laker Pregame Show from 1985–1991

It was most unusual for Chick, who wasn't one to back off.

"What do you think?" he asked the pilot.

"I don't like the way the sky looks," the pilot told him.

"Whatever you don't like, I don't like," Chick said.

And that was that. Hearn went back to his hotel and missed the Laker game.

The following evening, with Hearn again mikeside, the Lakers beat the Philadelphia 76ers 110–104 at the Los Angeles Sports Arena in front of 10,609 spectators.

With that broadcast, Hearn began a streak that spread through several generations of players, coaches, and listeners; an iron-man streak that Cal Ripken Jr. and Lou Gehrig could admire; a streak that defined Hearn; a streak that illustrated his work ethic, his fortitude, and his love of the game.

At first glance, Hearn's streak might not seem to belong in the same category with that of a Ripken or a Gehrig or an A. C. Green, who played in a record 1,192 straight NBA games. After all, Hearn wasn't an athlete whose streak could be threatened by concussions, sprained body parts, or all sorts of other breaks or bruises.

But Hearn had more than his share of ailments to overcome as the streak stretched into years and then decades. There were heart problems, prostate cancer, a knee injury, a damaged cornea, flu, colds, and that most dreaded of all health problems for an announcer, laryngitis.

But despite it all, when the Lakers would take the court, any court anywhere, there was Hearn behind the mike.

And the streak grew:

- His 500th straight Laker broadcast was a game vs. the Cincinnati Royals on January 14, 1971.
- 1,000[th]—Lakers vs. New York Knicks, April 8, 1977.
- 1,500[th]—Lakers vs. Seattle SuperSonics, February 16, 1982.
- 2,000[th]—Lakers vs. Utah Jazz, February 28, 1987.
- 2,500[th]—Lakers vs. Cleveland Cavaliers, March 13, 1992.
- 3,000[th]—Lakers vs. Orlando Magic, January 19, 1998.

MARGE HEARN

It never dawned on Fran to count the games. He didn't even know how many in a row he had until they told him it was a thousand.

And he didn't get serious about the streak until it reached twenty-five hundred. After that, he really wanted to keep it going. But he didn't brag about it. He was not one to do that.

———

On at least two occasions, Hearn ordered doctors to end blood transfusions so that he could get to a game.

SUSAN STRATTON
Hearn's Producer and Director for a Quarter of a Century

During the 2000–2001 season, we were in Houston when I got a call at our hotel from Marge on the day of a game. She was back home in L.A., but she told me she had talked to Chick and he was really sick.

We got him from his room, put him in a car, and took him to the emergency room of a nearby hospital. They ended up having to give him blood transfusions. It was related to the heart problems he would subsequently have. I left the hospital to go over to the arena, but I wasn't sure what was going to happen with Chick.

I had a car waiting for him because he insisted he was going to do the game.

Stu [Lantz] did the pregame show. And Chick showed up for the game. He had simply told the doctors that he couldn't continue the transfusion any longer. He had to go. Whatever they had given him would have to do. They removed the IV, and he walked out of there, went back to the hotel, changed his clothes, and there he was.

For those of us that knew him, you could hear it in his voice that night. It wasn't like it usually was, but it was incredible that he was even there.

When he made up his mind to do something, he was very bullheaded about it. But leave a hospital while having a transfusion? God, who would do that?

MARGE HEARN
He had several transfusions in L.A. before games in his last few years. I remember one time he was supposed to get two transfusions. Instead, he told me, "There's no time for a second one. Let's get out of here."

And we did.

———

Diagnosed with prostate cancer several years before he died, Hearn underwent successful radiation therapy, but managed to put it off until the off-season so it wouldn't affect his streak.

STEVE LOMBARDO
Laker Team Doctor
He had a pretty bad knee that he never told people about. About 10 years before his death, Chick had arthroscopic surgery during the season and never missed a game.

Prior to that, on the road, the knee got so bad that the doctor from the other team had to go to his room, drain the knee, and give him cortisone. He still made it to the game.

Chick was a real iron man, the Karl Malone of broadcasters. He had a passion for the game, a certain spirit that just propelled him. And it never diminished.

Except for the fact that his memory wasn't as good, he never missed a step physically until the end.

Susan Stratton

Before a game against the San Antonio Spurs in the Alamodome, I was in the truck getting ready when one of the guys came in and said, "Sue, Chick's outside in a cab. He wants you to come out."

He had scratched the cornea of his left eye while trying to remove a contact lens, couldn't see, and was in a lot of pain. I called the Spurs, got the name of their eye doctor, and one of the guys on our crew drove Chick over there.

The doctor treated him. About 6:30, he came back and went on the air. I don't know how he did that.

Joe Resnick
Associated Press

The Chick Hearn streak almost ended one night in 1995 because of blurred vision from that scratched cornea.

When I came into the Forum that night, I saw that they had set up his location courtside instead of his usual perch upstairs. There was no choice if Chick was to do the game that night, because he couldn't see from where he usually broadcast.

His courtside seat was only for that one game, his 2,703rd in a row, allowing his streak to continue.

Paul Sunderland
Hearn's Successor

There were probably a hundred occasions in 40 years where the streak was difficult to maintain. But when it was time to do the game, it was time to do the game.

STU LANTZ
Laker Broadcast Analyst

There were a number of times during my 15 years with the team that he shouldn't have been at work.

Two times, they took Chick off the air at halftime because he had laryngitis so bad no one could understand a word he was saying.

There were other times when you could understand him, but he had a cold or something and he felt terrible. Truly felt terrible.

But, when the light went on and the game was about to start, he went to work.

———

On March 5, 1994, Hearn was able to go on the air only hours after recovering from laryngitis. The next time, he wasn't so fortunate. On May 12, 1995, Hearn, again stricken with laryngitis, was unable to broadcast the second half of a playoff game against the San Antonio Spurs at the Forum. Lantz moved over to do the play-by-play, and a spectator named Magic Johnson agreed to step in and do the commentary.

On February 21, 2001, laryngitis again sidelined Hearn for the second half of a game, strangely enough also against the Spurs, this time in San Antonio. Lantz again became the play-by-play man and Derek Fisher, not playing that night, filled in as the analyst.

MITCH CHORTKOFF
Former Laker Beat Writer for the *Santa Monica Outlook*

It was Bob Steiner [the Lakers' public relations director] who had the chore of telling Chick that he couldn't broadcast the second half of that 1995 game.

Chick's streak of doing every game would still survive, even though he didn't finish. Didn't matter. Chick was livid, absolutely livid, for several days.

By our next stop in San Antonio, he seemed to have recovered. Trying to tiptoe around the subject, I gently asked how his voice was.

"I wasn't doing well," Chick said grudgingly, "and Bob Steiner correctly sent me home."

KOBE BRYANT
Laker Guard
My fifth year in the league, I had an injured ankle on a night when we were playing in San Antonio. Chick's throat was sore, and he couldn't announce the second half. So he sat in the locker room with me and watched the game. That was a lot of fun. He was still commentating the game, and I was getting a live show.

VIN SCULLY
Dodger Broadcaster
My longevity is God-given like his. The difference is, Chick had 82 games a year, we have 162. I knew very early in my career that I would welcome some days off. Chick, however, wanted that consecutive streak, and I admire him for it. I salute him if that's what he wanted. I'm so thrilled that he did it.

To be honest, that's the last thing I'd ever want is some consecutive streak of thousands of games. No, I like my time off.

———

The one man who can relate to the streak is the Dodgers' Spanish-language broadcaster.

JAIME JARRIN
Dodger Spanish-Language Broadcaster
I did almost four thousand Dodger games in a row. From 1962 until 1984, I didn't miss one single game. I stopped my streak because of the

Olympics. [Dodgers owner] Peter O'Malley was trying to get baseball to become a medal sport in the Olympics. He asked me to leave the Dodgers for three weeks in order to be in charge of the radio coverage of Olympic baseball. So I stopped my streak.

Having had such a streak, I can appreciate what it was for Chick to do that. He was older than I. Basketball is a faster game than baseball. In basketball, you only have one game in a city, and then you go to the next city.

RICK FOX
Laker Forward
I don't know how you can compare his streak to others. Cal Ripken Jr.'s streak, maybe. But Cal just had to show up. I'm sure he didn't play every one of those 2,632 games as well as Chick announced every game.

I always found it amazing that he was handling the travel at his age and handling it better than some of us.

ROSS PORTER
Dodger Broadcaster
Amazing. To do it in that sport where you're constantly jumping on airplanes, doing three games in a row in three different cities. You've got weather problems because the basketball season goes through winter. You've always got the threat of laryngitis.

And I never saw Chick worn out. He always kept his exuberance, his excitement.

~ 6 ~

His Players

Rare is the play-by-play announcer who is privileged to chronicle the era of a dynasty.

Rarer still is the play-by-play announcer who is privileged to chronicle the feats of superstars from several eras.

Rarest of all is the play-by-play announcer who is privileged to span the eras of two dynasties and enough superstars to fill a wing of the Hall of Fame.

Such an announcer was Chick Hearn.

He was the voice of the Lakers for nine championships, including a three-peat, a 33-game winning streak, a line of dominant centers ranging from Wilt Chamberlain to Kareem Abdul-Jabbar to Shaquille O'Neal, and a line of guards ranging from Jerry West to Magic Johnson to Kobe Bryant. Plus, Hearn spent his first few seasons covering Elgin Baylor in his prime. Air Baylor was soaring above NBA rims in spectacular fashion long before Air Jordan was launched or Dr. J. started practicing his trade.

Hearn wasn't about to single out a favorite from his galaxy of stars, but he did wear Baylor's warm-up jacket around the house for years, and he did think of West and Johnson as adopted sons.

SHAQUILLE O'NEAL
Laker Center

After my first championship, Chick pulled me aside and said, "I've been here through all of them, seen all the Laker centers. I even saw a little bit of [George] Mikan, and you're in my top two."

I said, "Well, who's first? Kareem?"

He said, "No, you're a little bit better than Kareem. I think Wilt's still a little ahead of you because Wilt did so much. But you are number two. Congratulations."

That was my best Chick moment. But there were many. Me and him used to talk a lot. He used to tell me old war stories about all the other centers.

His opinion of me meant so much because my thing is that, when you talk about this organization, I want to be recognized as the baddest big man. I know that's going to be hard because Mr. Chamberlain was a bad big man. But I think, if I keep doing what I'm doing, I'll be all right.

I also want to have more championships than Magic so I can be recognized as the baddest Laker of them all at any position. Right now, if someone brings their kids to a game and points at the retired jerseys on the wall, they say, "Well, son, that Magic Johnson had five championships, Kareem had five, Wilt had one, Jerry West had one."

If I get my way, they'll say, "That O'Neal, he got six."

If I can get the most championships, then I will be the best Laker to ever play basketball. And I would like to think that I became number one on Chick's list, too.

That's what I want, not only for me, but for my sons.

MITCH CHORTKOFF
Former Laker Beat Writer for the *Santa Monica Outlook*

When Chick was recovering from heart surgery, he came out for one game, sat in the press box, and, afterward, went in the locker room in a wheelchair. The players, who hadn't seen him in weeks, told him how great it was to have him back.

Shaq went up to him and said, "Chick, it's wonderful to see you. Is there anything I can do for you?"

"Yeah," said Chick, "get a damn rebound."

———

While O'Neal was already a superstar when he arrived in Los Angeles in 1996, Magic Johnson had yet to enjoy his first magical moment as a professional when Hearn first met him.

CHICK

He was something special right from the beginning. Magic Johnson was 19 years old when he came to the Forum after his sophomore year at Michigan State to meet Mr. Cooke. It was before the Lakers had signed him.

He came with his father, Earvin Sr., and his advisers, Dr. Charles Tucker and George Andrews. We all sat down to lunch.

"I'm going to order you some of our wonderful Forum fish," Mr. Cooke told Magic. "We are going to have sand dabs. They are m-a-a-r-r-rvelous."

———

Johnson picks up the story. . . .

MAGIC JOHNSON
Laker Player, Coach, and Part Owner

I was 19 years old. I didn't know what the hell sand dabs were, but I figured we'd see what happened when they came out.

Well, out came these brown pieces of fish. I took one bite and said, "I can't eat this." Cooke went crazy.

"What are you talking about?" he asked. "Do you know how much that fish costs?" He went on and on, telling me what a great fish it was and how expensive it was.

Finally, Chick, the one who had shown me around the Forum when we first got there, interrupted and said, "The guy's only 19. Only thing he knows is hamburger and pizza. You want a hamburger, Magic, right?"

I said, "Yeah."

"Bring him some hamburgers and french fries," Chick told a waiter.

When Jerry West got me outside, he told me, "You know, nobody has ever done what you just did to Jack Kent Cooke. And nobody has ever done what Chick did to Jack Kent Cooke."

Next we got down to the negotiating.

"What do you want?" Cooke asked.

"I want $430,000," I told him. "Plus, I want to finish my schooling, and I want you to pay for that schooling."

"I can't give you $430,000," Cooke said. "That means you'd be making more than Kareem. I can't pay you more than Kareem."

"Well," I said, "I guess I'll be going back to school."

Chick stepped in at that point and talked to my dad. Cooke was just a tough guy who was determined to get his way. But Chick was breaking it down, explaining the reason why they couldn't give me the money. It was a matter of team chemistry, he said, and the fact that the best player, Kareem, is supposed to get the most money. Chick went into the whole situation to help me and my dad understand.

Chick finished by saying, "Along with your salary, we're going to throw the college in, too."

At that point, my dad said to me, "Timeout. Let's go outside."

When we were alone, my father told me, "I don't care if they offer you $350,000. You are going to take it. In all my 30 years working at General Motors, I never made $400,000 or $350,000. You ain't turning this down."

I went back in and told Cooke, "Well, because of Chick and my dad, I'm going to take what you are offering."

I had agreed just because of Chick. I signed and the rest was history. So I was drawn to Chick that very first day.

Leaving Michigan, I was scared to death. Not the basketball part because I thought I could take care of that. But I'm from a family of 10 kids. We are close, so who was I going to turn to in L.A.? Where was I going to go?

It was Chick who became a powerful figure for me. He sort of saw a little son in me, and I saw a father figure in him. That's why I met him every morning for breakfast on the road with nobody else around. As we sat there, he took me through life's lessons. Those were, I think, my greatest moments with him, sharing his stories.

————

Treasuring private audiences with Hearn seems to be something Laker superstars over the years have in common.

KOBE BRYANT
Laker Guard

On the road, I would sit down and chat with him and Stu [Lantz] before the game. They were there doing their preparations, and I'd come out to shoot and work. It was amazing how on top of the game Chick was, even at that age. Still very witty.

All those Chickisms when we're talking about the game—I mean players, not just broadcasters or fans—they just come off our tongue as if they were invented with the game. No, Chick brought it to us.

He brought the game to life. That speaks volumes about the genius that was Chick.

JERRY BUSS
Laker Owner

One of the things that endeared me to Chick came right off the bat in my first year, also the year Magic joined the Lakers.

After about 40 games, I said to some of those around me, "You know, usually people don't recognize how great a player is until he's near retirement. So they really don't enjoy all his productive years. I want to explain to you that this is a legend you're watching. It's obvious, even though he's only played 40 games. So you should enjoy every game from here on out."

Everybody told me, "Wait a minute, he's just a rookie. You are going to have to wait five or six years."

It was Chick who said, "No, no, Dr. Buss is absolutely right. Magic will go down as one of the legends in basketball. Maybe *the* legend."

LON ROSEN
Sports Agent
There was a picture of Chick and Earvin that Chick really liked and wanted Earvin to sign. I remember Earvin took a lot of time to write something on that picture.

I gave it to Chick in his office at the Forum. I came back about two minutes later, and he was crying because it meant so much to him.

These players were really like his children.

––––––

And like any good father, Hearn taught his kids some of life's basic lessons, like beware of sucker bets—and one of the great free-throw shooters in NBA history, a man who led the league in free-throw percentage seven times.

MAGIC JOHNSON
Chick tricked me at my first training camp.

He says, "Maaag, I bet you can't beat Bill Sharman at free-throw shooting."

I'm thinking, what? I'm this hotshot kid, and Bill Sharman don't even play no more. OK, I'll take that bet. We bet five dollars, me and Chick.

Next thing I know, he's yelling out, "Sharman, get over here. This rookie wants to challenge you in free-throw shooting."

Chick is running the whole thing. "Let's have you shoot 20 each," he says. "Since you are the rookie, Maag, you go first."

I hit 14 or 15 of the 20, so I figure I'm about to win this five dollars. Then Sharman starts pumping them in. Swish, swish, swish. He hit the same spot every time. Swish, swish, swish When he got to 16 straight, I said, "You don't have to do it anymore."

When it was tears instead of laughter, Hearn was also there for Johnson.

At the start of the 1981–1982 season, the Lakers were becoming increasingly disgruntled over the offense being run by coach Paul Westhead.

While many players shared those sentiments, it was Johnson who spoke out, telling the media after a frustrating night in Utah that he wanted to be traded.

The subsequent uproar led to Westhead's firing. After Westhead's dismissal, Buss said that he had been about to make that decision even before Johnson's outburst. Still, even though he had been expressing the feelings of many of his teammates, Johnson became the bad guy in public, portrayed by many as a spoiled brat who got rid of the coach because he wasn't getting the ball enough. For a brief while the sparkle in Johnson's image faded as boos and hostility replaced the cheers and well wishes he had previously received around the country.

MAGIC JOHNSON

After the Paul Westhead thing, Chick gave me a big hug and told me I was wrong, but I was right. I was wrong for saying those things, but I was right for speaking up for the team. Chick said I should have only said it to Dr. Buss. "You just went about it the wrong way," he told me.

That wasn't the only time Hearn told Johnson he was wrong.

SUSAN STRATTON
Hearn's Producer and Director for a Quarter of a Century

Chick was very careful about not bothering the players. So I kept a list of everyone we asked to do anything to make sure we weren't asking anyone to do too much.

Magic had agreed to do an interview with us for halftime one night. I sent someone to the locker room to tell him we were ready. The person came back and told me Magic said he didn't want to do it.

This is kind of a problem at 6:15 on the night of a game.

I told Chick and he said, "Just a second."

He put the mike down and walked into the locker room. Next thing I know, here comes Magic. He sat down and did the interview.

When Chick and I were on the bus that night, I asked him, "How did you do that?"

He said, "I just told Magic I didn't think he was being fair. I told him I didn't ask him to do much, and I would appreciate it if he would come out and do the interview."

And Magic said, "OK."

Scott Ostler
Former Laker Beat Writer for the *Los Angeles Times*

It was Magic's rookie season, 1979–1980, and the team was in Seattle for its third game of the year. Magic had been playing great, galvanizing the team.

Sometime in the third quarter, he went down with a knee injury. Laying on the court, holding the knee, he was in obvious pain.

The following morning at the airport, waiting to catch a plane to the next city, everybody in the Laker party got the bad news at the same time. The Seattle team doctor, after looking at the X-rays, had determined that Magic had torn a knee ligament and could be out the rest of the season.

Back then, medical exams weren't as sophisticated. It turned out, of course, that the doctor was wrong. Magic was soon back on the court and would eventually lead the Lakers to the NBA title that season.

But it was a devastating blow at that moment at the airport. Chick was grief stricken. You couldn't talk to him. You couldn't go near him. He was almost in tears. It was like a death in the family. That's how much Magic meant to him, how much the team meant to him.

LON ROSEN

In 1991, 10 days before Earvin announced he was HIV positive, there was a lot of speculation about what was going on. We had held Earvin out of practice, saying he had the flu.

Chick didn't buy it. He kept calling me every day, asking me what was going on. He was very concerned. I kept telling Chick that there was indeed something going on and we were just trying to find out what it was.

Chick really loved Earvin. Remember, when Earvin joined the Lakers in 1979, Chick had been going through some tough years because the team wasn't doing well. They had sort of pushed Chick away from the job of assistant general manager and back to being just a broadcaster. So when Earvin rejuvenated the team, he and Chick formed a special relationship. Earvin always kept him informed about what was going on within the team. And Chick always kept that confidence.

When Earvin would have a video game, we would always ask Chick to do the voice. That meant a lot to Earvin.

About two or three days before we made the HIV announcement, I finally called Chick and told him what Earvin was about to reveal to the world. I knew you could always trust Chick with anything.

The news had a huge effect on Chick. He was in shock, stunned. He had no clue. Remember, this was back in 1991. HIV didn't enter into anybody's thought process back then if they were heterosexual.

After the announcement, Chick would call me almost daily for months. The question was always the same: how's Earvin?

———

Before there was Magic, there was Elgin.

ELGIN BAYLOR
Former Laker

We used to play gin rummy all the time, coast to coast, just to kill time on plane trips. Chick loved to play, but he never won.

I used to kid around and tell him, "You are probably letting me win so I get your per diem [money given to members of the team's traveling party for meals] and eat well. You just want to be sure I'm getting enough food."

On one plane trip, we were going to land in about 20 minutes. I flagged down a stewardess and asked her, "What would it take to get the pilot to circle for a couple more hours? I got a pigeon here."

He may not have been much of a card player, but Chick was a really good person. He showed me that in Boston one time when we were on our way out of town.

It turned out I had torn something in my stomach during the game, and by the time we got to the airport, I was in pretty bad shape. I was dehydrated and burning up with fever. I went outside where it was about 30 degrees, but I was still so sweaty that I had to take my coat off.

I came back in and went into the bathroom because I felt like I was going to vomit. Instead, blood came up. That scared the hell out of me.

When they announced our flight was boarding, I started walking to the gate, but I got so woozy, I felt like I was going to faint. First time I ever felt like that.

I told the coach, somebody called an ambulance, and they took me to a hospital. The team got on the plane, but not Chick. He stayed with me. He was concerned. He cared. That's the kind of loving person he was.

Fortunately, we had a break in the schedule, so neither Chick nor I were missing any games.

I was in the hospital for three days. They didn't know if they were going to have to perform surgery on me or what. I asked the doctor if what I had was serious, and he said, "Well, we've had a couple of people die from it, but they were like 70-something years old."

Chick remained there, came by to visit me every day.

Finally, I was released, and Chick and I got on a plane to come home. I looked at Chick as we sat down and said, "Now I get it. You probably figure this is the time you can finally beat me at gin."

We played all the way home from Boston, and I just hammered him.

FRANK O'NEILL
Former Laker Trainer

We would fly in the DC-8, which had a card table in front. Chick and Elgin would run up there at the start of a flight to get that table.

I remember one time, as they sat down, Chick handed Elgin a Christmas card. When Elgin opened it up, there was a check inside.

"What's this?" Elgin asked.

"It's my per diem check," Chick said, "to pay you what I owe from the last trip."

Those guys would gamble on anything. I remember Chick and Elgin standing at the baggage-claim area on every trip, betting whose bag would come off first.

———

When fans mentioned Baylor, West's name always seemed to follow. Within the Laker organization, however, Hearn's name was just as closely linked with both.

LON ROSEN

Chick and Jerry West, like Chick and Earvin, were like a father and son team. Back when Jerry played, they always looked after each other.

When Jerry decided he would go to Memphis [in 2002 to become president of the Grizzlies], I remember telling Chick. He was so happy for Jerry that he was coming back into basketball. Obviously, Chick would have preferred to have Jerry be back with the Lakers, but he was really happy for Jerry that he had found some happiness again in going back to work.

JERRY WEST
Laker Player, Coach, and Front-Office Executive
He was someone I know cared a lot about our team and about me. And I know what he did for the Lakers.

We were not having success artistically or financially when we first came to L.A. But Chick brought a different feel to a broadcast. It was more intimate, more personal. He changed the landscape for the sport in Los Angeles.

I think his success came from his thoroughness. His preparation for a broadcast probably rivaled that of a player, and it never varied all his years in Los Angeles.

———

Hearn didn't feel a closeness with all the players who wore the purple and gold.

SUSAN STRATTON
We were going to New York for a game against the Knicks in which Patrick Ewing would be making his inaugural appearance against Kareem.

A New York producer for the Knick broadcast called and asked if we were going to do anything with Kareem in advance. We had been planning on it, so I agreed to exchange interviews with the producer, who was going to interview Ewing.

Chick wasn't sure he wanted to do the interview because, if Kareem was in a bad mood, you could get yourself in deep trouble. I pleaded with Chick and he finally came around.

We were going to do the interview in Denver. When Kareem walked out onto the floor, Chick was waiting in a chair. Back in the truck, I heard Chick say into his microphone, "Uh-oh, this is bad."

He could tell by Kareem's demeanor.

Sure enough, to Chick's first two questions, Kareem answered simply, "Yes," and then, "No."

Finally, Chick asked, "Looking forward to playing this man so many people are comparing to you?"

"Don't know."

We couldn't run the interview. Nevertheless, I sent the tape on to New York with a note that said, "This is it, OK? This is all I got."

The New York people sent me a tape—they had crossed in transit—with a note that said, "Sue, sorry about this."

Marv Albert had done the interview with Ewing. When Albert asked him how he felt about playing Kareem, Ewing had said, "I don't know."

———

Hearn had an impact on so many players, but no one carries that impact around today more than "Big Game" James.

JAMES WORTHY
Former Laker

He gave me my nickname during the playoffs one year, and it has stuck longer and better even than my real name. Walking through airports wherever I am—East Coast, West Coast, or back home in North Carolina—people call me Big Game. And even more so in the last few years.

Whether I was fortunate enough to catch Chick in the morning on the road to have a cup of coffee, or at the bar at the Forum after a game, I considered it a moment to treasure.

RICK FOX
Laker Forward

When we talked, it was about other players who came before us and his thoughts on the current team. He was candid and honest. That's what I liked about our conversations. I like to be working with somebody who shares their feelings with you.

———

What amazed Fox was Hearn's ability to perform at the highest level despite the advancing years. Fox looked on in wonder as Hearn continued to maintain his self-imposed standard of excellence while continuing to zip around the country when most people his age had trouble zipping around their rest home.

RICK FOX

I don't know how you do that. Seriously, I don't know how he pulled that off.

In every walk of life, there are people who just stand out. It's something in their training or their chemical makeup. They have just been wired to do what they are doing and to do it better than anybody else. Just as there was a Michael Jordan or a Magic—these guys who were so special and stood out among all the other great players and were able to perform at such a high level—I don't know how you could match in Chick's field what he did for all the years he did it, and do it as great as he did and as consistently as he did.

DEREK FISHER
Laker Guard

He really made people feel that they were at the game. I remember Lakers-Sixers, Lakers-Celtics, Lakers-Blazers, all those series from when I was a kid. Now you watch NBA TV or you watch ESPN Classic, and Chick's doing the game. That makes me feel like I was a part of those series because I feel like he was a part of me, that we were both a part of this team together. It gives me an identification with those old Laker teams in all those old series.

———

Laker forward Kurt Rambis was a Hearn favorite, which also made him a favored target of Hearn's needling.

KURT RAMBIS
Laker Player, Assistant Coach, and Head Coach
When Chick spoke at a Laker event, he always seemed to wind up doing a mock play-by-play. He'd say, "Magic dribbling up the court, over to James Worthy. Slam dunk!"

But if there was one guy he was going to pick on, it would be me. So somewhere in that play-by-play, he'd say, "Rambis blows the layup."

But it was always in good fun. He'd end it by having me make the big shot.

LINDA RAMBIS
Kurt Rambis' Wife and a Member of the Laker Front-Office Staff
Chick would always, always, always tell everything about you on the broadcast, good and bad. You'd tell him something, and the next thing you know, there he is talking about it on the air. You'd tell him you were going to have company from out of town, and there he was, telling his audience, "So-and-so is coming to visit."

He announced the birth of our first child, Jesse Rambis. He was born on a night we were playing the Clippers. Chick announced the time of birth and all of that. I have a really fond memory of being in the hospital after having just delivered Jesse and hearing it on the broadcast.

You're thinking, "My gosh, my kid is so special that Chick is announcing it to the world."

But sometimes he would say something that you really wish he hadn't. For example, when Kurt was playing for the Phoenix Suns, the first time he came back to Los Angeles, I was taken to the hospital in Phoenix the same night because I was having a miscarriage.

Kurt was on the court when he was informed of my condition. Chick saw Kurt right after that, and Kurt was, obviously, still pretty disturbed.

Kurt and Chick had had a good relationship for many, many years. Chick was fond of Kurt—believed in him, the type of person he was. Chick saw the goodness Kurt added to the team. So when Chick saw Kurt that night, knowing him as well as he did, he could see how upset Kurt was. Chick naturally asked, "What's going on?"

Kurt told him. And Chick announced it on the air! Linda Rambis is having a miscarriage. If I had known, I would have told Chick, "No, don't say that. Don't say that."

After that, I heard from everybody.

But that was Chick. He really made all the players and their families part of the community. Fans came up to you and they really felt like they knew you. It was good. It was perfect because they came to think of us as regular people who have lives, go to work, have babies, have miscarriages, have things happen in their lives. It made it much more human. He really connected the players and their families, people to people, with the fans.

~ 7 ~

His Coaches

He went from Fred Schaus to Phil Jackson, from the contentious days of Bill van Breda Kolff to the glory days that began with Bill Sharman.

But of all the coaches who paced in front of him, none was closer to Chick Hearn than Pat Riley, who played in a Laker uniform because of him, broadcast beside him, and coached in front of him.

PAT RILEY
Former Laker Player, Broadcast Analyst, Assistant Coach, and Coach

Chick was always there at major turns in my life.

Before I knew much about the NBA, I knew about Chick Hearn. I knew his voice because Laker games were heard in San Diego, where I was playing for the Rockets. He had interviewed me, flattering me by calling me a great young player.

Our paths crossed again at a very difficult time in my life. I had been selected by the Portland Trail Blazers in the expansion draft, but I was trying to get out of there before I got cut. Having just come back from the funeral of my father, Lee, I was really down the night [in the fall of 1970] I bumped into Chick outside the Portland arena after a Laker-Trail Blazer preseason game.

I told Chick I wanted out of Portland, and he assured me, "You'll be in L.A. soon."

Whatever he saw in me, he convinced Fred Schaus, who was then the Laker general manager, and Joe Mullaney, who was the coach, that I would be right for the organization.

I owe Chick my career as a Laker, which lasted five years.

When I finally retired from the game because of a knee injury, after a year in Phoenix, I wanted to stay involved in the game. So I applied for several assistant coaching jobs with the major colleges around L.A. I figured, having played for the Lakers, I had a pretty good name in town. But they snubbed me, saying they didn't hire ex–NBA players.

————

When the position of analyst alongside Hearn opened up in 1977, Chick used his influence with the team to lure Riley back into the Laker family a second time.

And there Riley might have stayed, having thoroughly enjoyed the switch from the ball to the microphone, had not Jack McKinney tumbled over the handlebars of his son's bike, changing so many lives and fortunes.

It was November 8, 1979. McKinney was only 13 games into the job of a lifetime: head coach of a Laker team that included both Kareem Abdul-Jabbar and Magic Johnson.

McKinney had already installed the fast-break offense that would produce an exciting, entertaining style called "showtime" and result in the Laker dynasty of the eighties.

But McKinney wouldn't be around for any of that. He and his assistant coach and best friend, Paul Westhead, had made plans to play tennis on November 8, a rare day off. When McKinney realized his wife, Claire, had taken the family car, he hopped on his son John's bicycle for the mile and a half ride to the courts in Westhead's condominium complex on the Palos Verdes Peninsula.

What went wrong was never fully determined. But what is known is that McKinney, unable to stop while coming down a steep hill, flipped over, and, without the benefit of a helmet, cracked his head on the asphalt. He was found lying in a pool of blood.

At first it was assumed that Westhead would only be a temporary fill-in until McKinney recovered from his head injuries. A Shakespearean scholar, Westhead called himself the Lakers' "substitute teacher."

Every teacher needs an aide. Westhead looked up in the stands at the Forum and saw his. He asked Riley to fill Westhead's former role as assistant coach.

This was back in a simpler time, when one assistant was more than adequate. But Riley wasn't sure he wanted to be that one.

PAT RILEY

I had really gotten into broadcasting, and I didn't know if I wanted to go down there. I thought I'd be losing my spot.

But Chick told me, "This is a great opportunity for you to learn to be a coach. Then you can bring your coaching knowledge back to broadcasting. I will definitely keep your seat open."

––––––

Instead, of course, Hearn lost a broadcaster and the Lakers gained a record-setting coach. With the Lakers winning the championship that season under Westhead and McKinney still struggling to recover, Westhead kept the head job and Riley remained by his side.

When Westhead was fired late in 1981, Riley moved into Westhead's position and won four more titles with the Lakers.

Hearn may never have been a coach, but that never stopped him from giving advice to those who were.

FRED SCHAUS
Former Laker Coach and General Manager
One postseason we were heading down on a bus to Orange County for an intrasquad game while we awaited our next opponent in the playoffs.

We had a rule that nobody was to play golf during the season. And certainly not during the postseason.

As we were moving along, Chick was busy reading the *L.A. Times.* Suddenly, he spotted a story that Jerry West had had a hole-in-one the day before.

Chick announced it to everyone and asked me—I was then the coach—if I was going to fine or suspend West.

Boy, West was mad. He figured if it wasn't for Chick, he'd have gotten away with it.

I sure as hell wasn't going to suspend Jerry, but he got a fine.

PAUL WESTHEAD
Former Laker Coach

We were playing the Golden State Warriors in Oakland, and Chick was about two chairs from me. As best as you can, you try to focus on the game and not the commentary, but I was hearing him.

It was the middle of the third quarter. Larry Smith, a Warrior forward, got an offensive rebound, and Chick said, raising his voice, "Well, Laker fans, Larry Smith has more offensive rebounds than the whole Laker team. That is not a good sign, Laker fans."

And he was looking right at me. I was acting like I didn't know he was talking to me, but I got it. I got it. Chick would let you know what he was thinking, and I got the message.

In fact, I think I called a timeout and said, "Guys, we've got to do a better job of blocking out [for rebounds]."

And, by the way, we wound up winning the game.

———

Coaching from behind the microphone could cause problems. Did Jerry Buss ever think of trying to rein Hearn in?

JERRY BUSS
Laker Owner

I was tempted to. He would drive the coaches crazy by second-guessing them. And there were times when I thought I should ask him to maybe ease up on the coach a little bit, but I never did. No, I never did.

BILL SHARMAN
Laker Coach and Front-Office Executive

When I first became the Laker coach, I talked to Chick more than to anyone else. I'd ask what he thought of this player or that player. He studied so much and worked so hard that he knew everything about the league.

I give him a lot of credit for our winning the championship my first season [1971–1972], and especially our 33-game winning streak. That streak started in just the second week of the season. I was not yet that familiar with our players and what they preferred to do in certain situations. I was still trying to learn the personnel. And Chick really helped me. I'd ask him or he'd volunteer information about certain players, even those on other teams. And other coaches. Who ran the fast break well? What was the key play a team would turn to in a critical situation? What was the best way to defend against a certain club?

I'd ask him all sorts of questions. He didn't try to force himself on me. I went to him. And he was really helpful, really contributed to the success we had.

PAT RILEY

I never, ever let his comments on the air bother me. That's who Chick was. It wasn't malicious or hateful. He wasn't trying to blame anyone.

Yes, when I was coaching, I'd hear him say things like, "He didn't take a timeout when he should have. I can't believe he didn't take a timeout." Or he'd say, "It's time for Kareem to come back."

I never went back and said anything to him afterward. He was just doing his job, covering a game.

And there were so many times after games that [assistant coach] Bill Bertka and Chick and I would sit around at a bar or a restaurant, and Chick would say things that really helped me a lot. He knew a lot about basketball, about players, about their character. He had a lot of good opinions, and I listened to him.

Bill Sharman

Happy Hairston had a reputation for blowing layups. One night he was heading down the court for what appeared to be an easy layup.

It was in one of those arenas on the road where the broadcasters sit right next to our bench, and, sitting on the end, I could hear every word Chick was saying. And I heard him tell the audience, "Hairston blows the layup."

Now, he said that before Happy had even let go of the ball.

But, sure enough, he did blow the layup.

After the game, I asked Chick, "How did you know he was going to do that?"

Chick told me he knew the way Happy released the ball, and when it came off his hand in a certain unnatural way, as it did on that occasion, he was going to miss.

I never forgot that.

———

One of the disadvantages of having a courtside seat on the road was that Hearn ran the risk of having his vision blocked by a coach who wandered into his line of sight.

Yes, he understood that the adrenaline flowed on the sideline. Yes, he understood that coaches had more to worry about than Hearn's view of the game. But Hearn was, first and foremost, a broadcaster. And he couldn't broadcast what he couldn't see.

DEL HARRIS
Former Laker Coach

I stood up all the time. Early on, Chick yelled at me until he found out I was going to be up all the time. His name for me became "Del Harris, the upstanding coach."

I tried in general to keep out of his way when I could remember. Obviously, at home games, he was up higher and it wasn't an issue. But occasionally, on the road, he would be next to our bench. And I would occasionally block him out.

But you know Chick. To say what he wanted to say, he didn't have to actually see the game.

RAY STALLONE
Former Laker Statistician

Chick always held a pen in hand. One time in Milwaukee, while he was doing the play-by-play—he sat courtside there—several players came crashing into the broadcast table, causing Chick's pen to go flying onto the court. Pat Riley, who was then the Laker coach, reached down, picked the pen up, and put it in his pocket.

On the broadcast, Chick yelled, "Hey, that's my pen!"

I'm sitting there, saying to myself, "What are the listeners back in L.A. thinking when they hear Chick screaming that Riley's got his pen?"

———

Missing out on a play was bad enough. But missing out on information was even worse for Hearn.

BILL BERTKA
Laker Assistant Coach

When Riley was coaching, secrecy was an issue with him.

But if a guy wasn't going to play or a guy was hurt, if we had a change in our lineup for whatever reason and Chick didn't know about it in advance, you were gonna pay. I'm telling you. You would come to regret springing anything on Chick that he wasn't prepared for.

I'll never forget one year, when we were playing Boston in the NBA Finals, somebody got hurt and wasn't going to play, and, for whatever reason, Pat said, "Don't tell Chick."

Today, the league has rules about disclosing injuries, but at that time, you didn't have to reveal what a player's status was.

But I avoided Chick. I didn't go into the elevator, I didn't go into the coffee shop, I didn't go anywhere he might be because I didn't want him to ask me about that player. I wasn't about to lie to him.

He finally asked somebody—I'll leave the name unsaid—and they did what Pat had instructed us to do: they avoided the issue.

When Chick finally found out, jumping catfish, he was beside himself!

After the game, Pat, myself, and Dave Wohl, another assistant coach, were at a hotel bar and here comes Chick. I could see he was on fire. I just cringed.

"Don't you guys ever, ever do that again," he told the three of us. "Don't you ever withhold that kind of information from me. I'll never forgive you if you do that again."

I didn't say anything. I just gave Riley that I-told-you-so look.

~ 8 ~

His Organization

Working for Jack Kent Cooke could be a terrorizing experience.

"HOT" ROD HUNDLEY
Former Laker Player and Broadcast Analyst

I was scared to death of the man. I remember one day he came through the offices at the Forum, throwing books on everybody's desk without saying a word.

The title of those books was something like *How to Work 24 Hours a Day*.

In Cooke's years with the team, Chick Hearn was the only one who never had to worry about being fired. Everybody else—general managers, coaches, players, front office—had to worry. Cooke fired people left and right. He had no heart. But not in Chick's case. Chick was safe because he was the greatest Laker of them all, and Cooke knew it.

————

And Hearn knew he had more latitude with Cooke than everyone else in the organization.

FRANK O'NEILL
Former Laker Trainer

Even though the Laker colors were purple and gold, Cooke insisted Chick say the colors were Forum blue and gold. But Chick continued to call them purple and gold.

87

When Jerry Buss bought the team in 1979, Hearn still didn't have to worry. His new owner was also a longtime admirer of the Laker announcer.

JERRY BUSS
Lakers Owner
I had always listened to Chick because I was a big Laker fan. One of the reasons I bought the team was because I couldn't get good tickets.

And in Hearn's later years, when Jeanie Buss, a daughter of the Laker owner, took over much of the responsibility for the day-to-day operation of the club, Hearn found yet another fan

JEANIE BUSS
Laker Executive Vice President of Business Operations
From a marketing standpoint, having Chick as part of this franchise meant that we would always have something to sell.

The players were going to come and go, retire or be traded, or become free agents. But Chick was a star himself, and people like him are few and far between.

Growing up in L.A., I knew who he was prior to my dad owning the team. I knew him from *Bowling for Dollars* [a television program].

Then my father bought the Lakers, and I had an opportunity to meet Chick. He could make you feel like the most important person in the world. He always remembered my name and what I was doing. He was just one of those people who could make you feel special.

It meant a lot to me that he was a part of my career.

MARY LOU LIEBICH
Laker Administrative Assistant

Chick was an absolute perfectionist, and he had no room in his life for anyone who wasn't.

When I first came here, Chick was assistant general manager under Mr. Cooke. There had to always be at least one executive in the office during working hours, even in the summertime, despite the fact that there wasn't as much going on during the off-season as there is these days.

When Pete Newell was the general manager, he always took a month in the summer and went to Japan. Chick had to come in every day in Newell's absence.

Chick's office was right next to mine, and he would call out to me, "Mary, whatcha doing?"

"Oh, not much."

In those days, we didn't do as much scouting, we didn't have summer league to the extent we have now, and the whole free-agent thing wasn't like it is now.

Chick would say, "Let's talk."

"OK, whatcha want to talk about?"

"Oh, anything." So we would proceed to talk, and not necessarily about basketball. Chick was so used to being active that when nothing was going on, he was bored.

———

It wasn't quite the same in the Buss era.

JERRY BUSS

When I came to the Lakers, Chick was the assistant general manager and traveling secretary, and there were a lot of other things he used to do. But, as the organization grew, we realized we could afford people to take some of the load off his shoulders.

Still, even when he wasn't assistant general manager anymore, when I would talk to Chick, he would voice his opinion very strongly. He would tell me, we need a shooter, we have to have a backup center, we gotta do this, we have to do that.

He absolutely gave me his opinion many, many times. And sometimes, we followed it.

Mary Lou Liebich

When he no longer had the duties of assistant general manager, Chick still wanted to be involved.

During the summer he would call me every day just to chat. He would say, "Mary, what have we done today? Who are we going to get? What do you hear? How many people do you think they are going to go into training camp with? Who are they going to bring in?" He couldn't stand not being in the middle of things.

If anything happened that you had not called him about in advance, he would be really irritated, politely irritated. If he heard the Lakers were considering someone, he'd call me to find out why I hadn't told him.

"Chick, they haven't even signed him yet," I'd say. "He is supposed to be in tomorrow, but I'm not supposed to say anything."

Chick would say, "Well, you know you can tell me."

When he was in charge, Jerry West was very strict about giving out information to anyone, including Chick. I was between the devil and the deep blue. Bill Sharman was more lenient when he was general manager.

Chick would be upset for maybe a few minutes if I hadn't told him something, then we'd get on with the conversation. He never got mad at me. He understood my position, what I could tell him and what I couldn't tell him, but he never really accepted it.

MITCH KUPCHAK
Laker Player and General Manager

Chick was very mindful of my position. He would never tell me what to do, or what he thought. But by the end of the conversation, even though he didn't come right out and say it, I knew exactly how he felt, exactly where he stood.

Sometimes I'd ask him for an opinion about a player and he'd say, "Well, I really don't have an opinion." And then he'd be quiet. That meant he didn't like the player.

It was the same thing if I asked him about a coach.

In the time he was here, Chick's presence grew to the proportions of a John Wooden. Chick was so revered in this town that it kind of took on a life of its own.

Players and coaches who came to Los Angeles and didn't know who Chick was quickly caught on.

———

So did trainers.

GARY VITTI
Laker Trainer

When I interviewed for the job as Laker trainer, Jerry West told me about Chick—warned me about him. Jerry said, "We got a guy who likes to needle people. He'll say things on the air about you. I hope you are not too sensitive."

"Now that you told me," I said, "I'll be OK. Otherwise, I might have worried about it."

So we go to training camp at College of the Desert in Palm Desert. Chick is sitting up on that stage that overlooked the court. It's my very first day, I'm running around trying to get things organized, and he starts yapping at me from that stage. I haven't even met him yet, but he knows who I am and he's yapping away.

So I answer back, "Go ahead and say what you've got to say. I've already heard about you."

He starts laughing because somebody had come back at him, and from then on, we were friends.

It turned out there was a whole sentimental side to him. He cried when I told him I was getting divorced from my wife, Christine. Really cried. He cared about her as a person. He didn't talk to me after that for a while.

FRANK O'NEILL

Chick was the first announcer to introduce a trainer to the radio audience. People began to recognize who I was, all by virtue of Chick.

He got so involved in diagnosing injuries on the air that we started calling him Dr. Hearn and presented him one time with a stethoscope and a black bag.

CLAIRE ROTHMAN
Former Executive Under Both Jack Kent Cooke and Jerry Buss

I called him Chicklet.

During his broadcasts on the road, if a scoreboard went out, if a floor was wet, if it took a long time to replace a net for a basket, if there was any disruption in the play, Chick would use the occasion to give me a boost. He would say, "This would never happen in a building run by Claire Rothman. She would have had it fixed long before this."

LAWRENCE TANTER
Laker Public-Address Announcer

When I started in 1982, I realized there was no barometer to judge my craft. I was one of only 24 guys doing it. I didn't want to be another Dave Zinkoff, the Philadelphia guy who was the predominate public-address announcer at the time. I wanted to be different.

So I went up to Chick and said, "You've been traveling around the league all these years, listening to different public-address announcers. How do you think I should sound?"

Chick told me, "Try to imagine you are talking to a blind person. In other words, try to be very precise, correct, forthright with your verbalization. Always keep in mind that you are communicating with that blind person."

I did, and it worked for me. It made me very cognizant of the information I was disseminating because I am, in effect, an extension of the officials.

I really appreciated that from Chick, because he didn't have to do that.

After that, he and I would always tease each other before the game. I would say to him, "Where's your blind person sitting tonight?"

––––––

It wasn't just members of the Laker organization who got the benefit of Hearn's mastery of communication skills.

MARY LOU LIEBICH

People would call in and want to do an interview with Chick, especially people who wanted to follow in his footsteps, or college students who had to interview someone in the business. And Chick was always really, really good about doing those interviews.

I would set them up. If, for instance, that night's game was at 7:30, he would have the person come in at 4:30. Chick would be there at 2:00, do what he had to do, and then he would allocate that time at 4:30 for the interview. But you'd better be on time.

He would take people at their word that this interview was something they had to do, some assignment. He didn't have me check up on them.

ISAAC LOWENKRON
L.A. Radio Reporter

I was a junior at SC in the fall of 1999. There was an unveiling party for this Kobe Bryant video game, and the deal was, Chick was going to be there listening to student announcers and giving out broadcasting tips.

Chick and Marge walked in, and I first started talking to Marge. Chick came over and Marge said to him, "I want to introduce you to this young man. He wants to be a basketball announcer."

At that point, being only 19 and actually meeting him, I almost fainted from excitement.

Because there was still plenty of time before the event began, Chick spent the next half hour, just him and me, giving me advice on being a basketball announcer.

When he talked to me, there was an incredible amount of sincerity in his eyes, as if you were a member of his family.

It was like getting advice on writing from Shakespeare. It was like talking music with Mozart. It was a once-in-a-lifetime opportunity.

The thing that struck me most was how fundamentally sound his philosophy was. There weren't a lot of tricks. It was just old-fashioned hard work. He was big on accuracy. Know the rules, he told me. Keep a rule book with you. Know the pronunciation of the players' names.

"When I say, it is an 18-foot shot, do you know how I know it was an 18-footer?" he asked me. "Because I went out on the court and measured that distance."

Then it came time for the video demonstration, and I was one of those doing the play-by-play. I was extraordinarily nervous, but I thought I was doing pretty good.

Chick was sitting next to me. When we got about three minutes in, he said, "Hold it!"

I thought, "Oh no."

He said, "You haven't given the score or the time of the game in the last two minutes. I'm driving down the freeway in my car, and I'm ready to kill you. The thing that people want to hear the most is the score. The only person who cares about you when they're listening to a game is your mom."

ROY ENGLEBRECHT
Founder of Sportscasting Camp

I paid Chick $200 to come to my camp in Santa Barbara, and I got more than my money's worth. I figured he'd tell war stories, but he turned into a college professor. It blew me away.

This was a guy who was very proud of his profession and wanted to tell eager young people how he did it. He didn't just tell stories. He broke down play-by-play, how to prepare, what to read, what to call the different areas of the court, even what to drink if your throat is giving you problems. I would have been happy with one hour, but he gave me two and a half to three.

He listened to the campers' tapes and stayed around to sign autographs.

What I saw was a really, really caring side of Chick, someone who wanted to give something back. It was not just a speaking appearance. These were people who wanted to make a living in the profession Chick loved, and he wanted to help them do so.

He spoke at that camp for six years. One day a year, Chick Hearn would turn into a college professor.

———

Hearn knew what he needed for a successful broadcast. When he didn't get it, he certainly wasn't hesitant about speaking up.

LEE ZEIDMAN
Arena Operations Director

In the early nineties, we had that archaic scoreboard at the Forum that was literally kept lit at the end with Christmas tree bulbs. Back then, we used to drop the 24-second shot clocks down by a line from the catwalks. The clocks weren't on the baskets because they were archaic as well.

We finally put a new scoreboard in one summer, a great-looking scoreboard, huge.

The first game, Chick called me up to his perch along the western sideline.

"There's a major problem here," he told me.

"What do mean, Chick?" I asked. "You've got a brand-new scoreboard. You've got video replay, which you didn't have before. This is great."

"Sit here," he said, motioning to his chair.

"So what's the problem?" I repeated after I sat down.

"What do you see?"

"I see a beautiful scoreboard with everything on it."

"I can't see the 24-second clocks," he told me. "How am I supposed to call the game? You got to do something."

The clocks were on top of the baskets, similar to what we have now at Staples Center, but Chick, even tilting his head, couldn't see them.

"All right, here's what we'll do," I told him. "We'll tape white all around the 24-second clocks to frame them out. That way, you'll be able to pick them up better and they won't get lost in the crowd."

We did that, but the next day, he called me up again. "I still can't see them," he said. "Not going to work for me. I can't call the games without the 24-second clock."

By that point, Chick was starting to talk about it on the air.

I had to go back to the company that made the scoreboard and tell them the only thing that was going to solve the problem was to put a 24-second clock on the very top of the scoreboard.

And that's what we did.

The clock was facing him. Nobody else but Chick could see it. All he had to do was look up at the scoreboard. We kept it that way when we moved to Staples Center.

And, to this day, I believe it's the only 24-second clock that is on the top of the scoreboard in any arena in this country.

Hearn was comfortable in the Forum. Who wouldn't be after calling a place home for nearly 32 years?

But in 1999 the Lakers moved to a new home, Staples Center. And like any longtime resident being uprooted, Hearn had his concerns about the shift.

MICHAEL ROTH
Staples Center Vice President of Communications

During the construction of Staples Center, there was a question whether Chick would be on the floor, like he is in most other arenas. Chick did not want to be there, so we carved out a special area for him.

Although construction was under way the summer before the arena opened, Chick hadn't been there yet. At that point, there had been a tightening of the security operation because they had been lax about letting people onto the site.

I was down there one Saturday morning at about 10:00, and, lo and behold, I see in the distance Chick Hearn, Marge Hearn, and two security officers walking out of the construction site.

Not only did Chick not have a hard hat on, but he was in shorts.

I couldn't believe this had happened. Chick had just walked up and the security people had offered to take him in.

He pulled me aside and, it was obvious, he was a little annoyed.

"Michael," he said, "this just isn't right."

"What do you mean?" I asked him.

"The spot they built for me. I can't broadcast from there."

What had happened was that the security officer had taken him to the wrong place—not to the basketball press box, but to the one to be used for hockey. That press box is about three stories higher than the one designed for Chick.

I took him back in, with a hard hat this time, to show him where his broadcast place was going to be, and he felt much better.

————

When Staples Center opened a few months later, there was the comforting sight of Hearn, as he had been at the Sports Arena and the Forum, now in a new broadcast perch, ushering his Lakers into yet another era.

~ 9 ~
His Family

They were together for 68 years, married for 63. They shared the unbelievable exhilaration of rising from small-town beginnings to big-city fame and fortune. They shared the unimaginable tragedy of losing both their children.

Through it all, Chick and Marge walked side by side with a love that endured those twin tests of time and trauma.

She knew him when he was a 17-year-old basketball player and an 85-year-old basketball broadcaster. She laughed at his jokes, hung on his every broadcast word, and shared his sorrow.

And he responded, paying her tribute in a myriad of ways, even sometimes as the object of his good-natured one-liners.

JEANIE BUSS
Laker Executive Vice President of Business Operations

Because Chick was always talking about Marge, every Laker fan felt they were on a first-name basis with her. That was inspiring to so many people. You just don't see that kind of dedication in a relationship anymore. I would love to find a relationship like that of Marge and Chick. They just truly enjoyed each other's company and would always be together.

DYAN CANNON
Actress

Marge was his mistress because he was married to the game. That was his oneness.

The thing that moved me most about Chick, if I had to sum it up in one word, was integrity. That integrity allowed him to understand, master, and teach what the game of basketball was all about.

And that was the same way he approached his marriage. You never heard stories. These guys were traveling on the road all the time. A woman thinks about those things. But never, in all the years Chick was around, was there anything in terms of rumors or gossip about him. The man lived a life of honor.

MARY LOU LIEBICH
Laker Administrative Assistant

Marge was Chick's life. She was his soul mate. They did everything together. Now, there were times during the summer when she'd say to me, "Mary, can't you speed up the time until the new season? I need to get him out of the house."

That was said in jest because they probably had the strongest relationship of anyone that I've ever known.

MYCHAL THOMPSON
Laker Player and Broadcast Analyst

Whenever our plane was pulling onto the tarmac at the end of a road trip, Chick was in such a hurry to see Marge that he couldn't wait for the plane to come to a stop. He would get up out of his seat, walk to the front of the plane with his bag, and stand by the door.

I was surprised he even waited for them to bring the steps up. He looked like he was going to just jump out the door when it was opened.

He was that anxious to get home and see his lovely Marge.

BOB KEISSER
Long Beach Press-Telegram Media Critic

Every time I talked to Chick for a TV column, he always seemed to include Marge in the conversation.

When he was in his sixties and people were saying that maybe he should retire, he'd say, "I still think I'm doing as well as I have ever done. I still think I'm sharp. I still break the tape down every night with Marge."

You are talking about a 60-year-old guy who had been in the business 40 years breaking down a tape with his wife. There are guys half his age who don't break down tapes.

———

They certainly don't get as much publicity as their celebrated husbands, but the Laker wives have also been a force in the community for a long time, a force for charitable organizations and other worthwhile causes.

And the wives always knew that Marge was their most valuable asset.

Jeanie Buss
What was brilliant about Marge was that, whatever event or product we were trying to sell to raise money for our various charities, she would make sure Chick was as passionate about the project as all the Laker wives were.

That's why all those projects were so successful. He talked about them with such feeling that it wasn't just someone reading an announcement. You knew it meant something to him because it meant something to Marge.

Linda Rambis
Kurt Rambis' Wife and a Member of the Laker Front-Office Staff
I remember when I was in the Lakers wives' group that Marge would just badger Chick to sell our things on the radio. They didn't have time for any advertisers because, every two seconds, it was sell the cookbooks, sell the calendar, sell this, sell that.

At one point, someone in the Laker office said, "This is all fine and dandy, but we have advertisers we are obligated to."

But Chick didn't care. His wife was on his back, so he was going to do it.

———

But there was a trade-off for Marge. While she knew she could always use her husband to further her causes, she knew he would use her, in turn, in the punch line of many of his jokes.

She didn't mind, not even when she had to listen to the same joke over and over again at banquet after banquet, roast after roast.

John Ireland
L.A. Sportscaster

The Lakers would do a Chamber of Commerce luncheon every year just before the start of the regular season. It was always a huge affair.

One year, the team showed up late, but even after they arrived, people continued to stand around and drink cocktails. Those in charge wanted to get the whole thing over with by 1:30. The Lakers had to go practice, and people had to get back to work.

But nobody was sitting, and the people in charge were starting to panic.

Finally, someone came up to Chick and told him, "Go up to the microphone and get people to sit down."

So Chick got up and said, "Ladies and gentlemen, welcome. Glad you could come. My lovely wife Marge is here, and, as you can see, she's wearing a lovely hat."

With that, Marge got a smattering of applause.

"Ladies and gentlemen," Chick continued, "I need you to sit down. We need to be out of here by 1:30 because Marge rented that hat."

———

Chick once received a free cruise as a gift, but it was in the steerage section. Asked where he was going on his cruise, Chick replied, "As far as Marge can row."

When asked why he spent so much time in his backyard, Chick replied, "When Marge is cleaning the pool, she can only work 30 minutes at a time."

MARGE HEARN

I didn't mind because he was always joking around. It was never a downer to be around him. I remember when we first got married, he said my meals knocked the bottom out of the garbage pail.

But he actually loved my chili, believe it or not.

When it came to meals, Fran had a routine. After he and Stu [Lantz] would record the pregame show, Fran would move to a deserted part of the arena—remember, he had already been there four hours—whip out his can of Slim Fast, and enjoy some brief quiet time. After a home game, we'd drive back to the house and Fran would unwind with a drink and a plate of macaroni and cheese.

He always seemed to want me beside him, even when he was just trimming a bush.

He enjoyed yard work and just sitting out on the patio, enjoying the gorgeous view we had of the San Fernando Valley from our Encino home. He loved doing crossword puzzles, going to the theater, and playing golf.

He usually played at Wilshire Country Club, eventually getting down to a 5 handicap, although he always said it was really a 7. Bing Crosby and Phil Harris still owed him money when they died from the bets they used to have on the golf course.

I only played with him once, in a husband and wife tournament. I wound up with a 9 on one hole, and that was the end of our golf partnership.

———

Hearn's needling of Marge was all for laughs—the only people who could even come close to competing with her in his eyes were his kids, Gary and Samantha, and later his granddaughter, Shannon, and great-granddaughter, Kayla.

Hearn was so anxious to see the birth of his son in 1942 that, despite the fact that World War II was raging, he was able to delay his induction into the service for several months to help usher his son into the world.

Family was always important to Hearn.

BILL DWYRE
Los Angeles Times Sports Editor

Chick's mother and my grandmother on the maternal side were sisters. In my family, if you were in the newspaper business, you'd be told, "Well, maybe someday you'll be as good as Chick Hearn." He was on this pedestal and I was always kind of in awe. When he would come through town, we would talk.

In 1972 I was at the *Milwaukee Journal* when my mother, Mary, called up and said she wanted to bring Aunt Dodee, who was at least in her seventies and from the Illinois side of the family, to the Milwaukee Bucks game that night. The Bucks were playing the Lakers, who had won 33 in a row.

So these little old ladies come to see Chick and this is the game where the Lakers lose to end the streak.

It was one thing for Chick to sit with them after the game if the Lakers had won to make it 34 straight. It was another thing when the streak ended.

Chick was doing all this postgame stuff, and there were these two ladies and he's got to do the family thing. But he was wonderful. He was just wonderful. I could see he was really mad about the loss. He took it very seriously. You want to keep the streak going.

But he sat down with them and talked to them, and they all went off and had a cup of coffee somewhere and chatted about the old days in Peoria. I saw Chick and these two little old ladies going off into the distance after that big game and I just thought, "He has to be a saint." I don't know how he did it.

When my mother died, my sister went through all these old pictures taken using a tripod. They were in the Peoria and Aurora area. I took a bunch of them and went over to Phoenix—I covered the Laker game there that night—and I saw Chick before the game.

We sat down courtside with the pictures. I'd say, "That's so-and-so," and he'd say, "No, that's Aunt Aggie. That's a different side of the family. Look at that stupid hat." I think he was even in a couple of those pictures himself as a little kid.

He really enjoyed reminiscing about those days.

———

When the Hearns made the move from Peoria to Los Angeles, Gary was 14, Samantha 9. They were entering their formative years in a brave new world.

MARGE HEARN

Gary was a great basketball player while we were still living in Peoria. They let him practice with the high school team when he was still in the eighth grade.

He grew to be 6'5", witty, and handsome. Gary had Fran's sense of humor, but more so. He loved people and they loved him. When Gary walked into a room, he took over. His charisma was like Magic's.

Gary served two years in the armed forces in Germany. When he got out, he worked as an extra in the movies. He also kept stats for his father at Laker games and worked as a bartender.

Around that time, he met a girl named Beverly. They married and had a daughter, Shannon. But Gary and Beverly divorced while they were still in their early twenties.

SHANNON HEARN-NEWMAN
The Hearns' Granddaughter

My friends always asked what it was like growing up with Chick Hearn. I was so young, it wasn't until I was an adult that I realized the impact that it had on all our lives, and the privileges that came with it. To me, it

105

was just part of growing up. That was just his job. When you're born into it, you don't think of it as that unusual.

I remember when I was about three, I was at a Laker game with my grandmother at the Sports Arena. Just when they were ready to start, I got away from her and started running down the floor to where my grandfather was sitting. When I reached him, I leaned into his microphone and said, "Hi, Grandpa." That was as far as I got because, by then, my grandmother had gotten to me.

Sometimes, when I got a little older, I would even be allowed to sit next to my grandpa during games if I was really, really quiet and he was in a really, really good mood. I sat there the whole game as long as I didn't make a sound. It was just cool. It was the best seat in the house.

And sometimes I was allowed to go out on the court and shoot baskets during practice. I had so much fun at the Forum, growing up, hanging out with my grandpa. I had the run of the place. An usher would tell me, "You can't go there," and I'd say, "Excuse me, do you know who I am?"

I remember my grandparents being so happy, my grandpa being so loving toward everybody. He was very sensitive. He was the kind who could read a birthday card and start crying.

I remember my dad as this larger-than-life guy.

My grandmother has told me about the funny kind of trouble he would cause. Like the time he wanted an alligator. So he got one and put it in my grandparents' pool.

They had this big, green Cadillac that my dad didn't like. One day, when they came home, they found he had spray painted one whole side of it with the words "The Green Hornet" in yellow paint.

CHICK

When the Lakers won their first championship, in 1972, Gary was sitting with Marge. I still have a vivid memory of Gary shooting up out of his seat, racing up to where I was telling the basketball world the Lakers had won, and squeezing my hand.

Just a month after the peak moment of the Lakers' years in Los Angeles to that point, the Hearns were plunged into a valley from which they never fully recovered. It was June 1, 1972, a family day around the pool. Chick and Gary swam together.

Late in the afternoon, Gary said he was going out for cigarettes.

CHICK
We never saw him again.

The next day, Gary wad found dead of a drug overdose in the back seat of a car parked on a street in North Hollywood. He had needle marks on one arm.

Gary Hearn was 29.

MARGE HEARN
From that day on, all our lives changed.

SHANNON HEARN-NEWMAN
We were the perfect family on the outside, but there was trouble on the inside.

MARGE HEARN
Gary had said to me, "I'm in trouble," not long before his death. He wanted out of that trouble, and we tried every way we knew to help him. It was the end of the hippie era, when drugs were so prevalent. Many parents were not aware of how to deal with that. At first, we didn't know what to do, but we soon got him into a state hospital for treatment.

Gary was born 30 years too soon. Today, with all the rehab clinics, he would have had a chance.

CHICK

We think what happened that night was that he ran into some of his old buddies and they offered him the drugs. I think afterward they just got scared.

MARGE HEARN

We were never able to say good-bye. I'm positive he wanted to come back. We were hoping one of his friends would at least call us and tell us what happened. But none of them ever did.

SHANNON HEARN-NEWMAN

I was nine years old. My mother picked me up from school and told me what had happened. It was horrible, horrible, horrible.

———

The depth of Chick's grief can be measured by the depth of his devotion to his only son. That's illustrated in a letter Chick sent to Gary on his second birthday. Serving in New Caledonia in the midst of World War II, Chick wrote:

> I realize that if I and all the other men serving around me, and those serving in Europe, do a good job now, then you will never need to be separated from those you love, such as has happened to me. To spare you that, Gary darling, I'd gladly give my very life.
>
> To date, son, we haven't had the time nor the good fortune to see each other and really commence the powerful bond of love and devotion that will exist forever between you and me.
>
> Naturally, I know that you are too young to know how much all this will mean to each of us in years to come, but, sure as God made little green apples, I'll be the very best dad to you that any boy has ever known.
>
> In closing, I merely want to tell you that, since the day of your conception, your mamma and daddy have been made very, very

happy. I pray that Almighty God will see fit for me to once more be with you and bring to you whatever happiness a good father can bring to a son he loves so dearly.

CHICK

I had been offered the *Bowling for Dollars* television show but had turned it down. But after Gary died, I called and asked if the job was still open. If I didn't work, I felt like I would just sit around thinking and go crazy. It was work and prayer that has gotten me through it.

MARGE HEARN

I think working saved his life.

MARY LOU LIEBICH

I first came to work for the Lakers just shortly after Gary had passed away. I remember walking by Chick's office and he would be sitting at his desk, looking at Gary's picture.

And the tears would just be streaming down his cheeks.

STU NAHAN
L.A. Sportscaster Who Later Became the Channel 4 Sports Anchor

In 1982 I lost a daughter, Marcy. She swallowed her tongue while she was sleeping. Just 20 years old.

The next year I was covering the Lakers in the NBA Finals against the Sixers. The first two games were in Philadelphia, and I remember Chick getting ahold of me in the lobby of our hotel.

He put a heavy hand on my shoulder and said, "Can I talk to you for a minute?"

"Stu," he said, "I know what you're going through because I lost one of mine. A parent is not supposed to lose a child and the pain will never go away. But I guarantee you, Stu, as the years go by, the pain will lessen. Listen to what I'm saying now: you are going to be OK and your daughter is in a better place."

I will never forget what he said to me that day in that Philadelphia hotel.

———

After Gary's death, Shannon moved in with her grandparents and they tried to resume some semblance of a normal home life.

SHANNON HEARN-NEWMAN

My grandparents were like my parents at that point.

We'd have these aluminum can drives at school, and my grandfather would have everybody at the Forum collecting cans. We'd walk into the Forum hallway after the game and there would be dozens of those green trash bags full of aluminum cans. My grandfather would tie them all together and drag them out to his car.

We'd win every aluminum can drive. We'd have more cans than anybody.

Those days in the Forum press lounge after the games in the mid-seventies with Gale Goodrich and Jerry West and all the rest there, those were the best years of my life.

After every game, my grandfather would go behind the bar and pour everybody drinks. He was the bartender. That was how he relaxed. All the wives and friends would be in there and it was like this big family party after every game.

———

Samantha Janis Hearn was a natural athlete who competed in swimming, basketball, volleyball, and softball. Swimming was her best sport, the butterfly her specialty. She became so good in the pool at such a young age that her parents were approached about a training program for the Olympics.

Chick in front of his own popcorn machine, in honor of one of the many unique Chickisms he coined.

Throughout all the years and all the games to go "in the fridge," Chick goofed one time by declaring the game over a little too soon; the Lakers actually blew the lead and the game.

Chick celebrates his star on Hollywood's Walk of Fame with family and friends in 1986.

Lasting friendships from the Lakers' fabulous run during the eighties included the incomparable Magic Johnson (above) and the unflappable Pat Riley (below).

Chick helped Lakers fans salute one of their heroes when he emceed James Worthy's retirement ceremony at the Forum.

Another dear friend from the Lakers family was the one and only superfan, Jack Nicholson.

Chick and Jerry West were both Lakers lifers, having spent practically their entire professional lives with the organization.

Chick's last championship parade in Los Angeles, following the 2002 title run.

As it should be, Chick is included among the Lakers immortals.

Chick's home away from home, where he could literally sit amongst the fans and call the games alongside them.

Chick and Marge with their "boys" in 1990.

MARGE HEARN
Sammy declined because she didn't want to devote her whole life to one thing.

————

For Samantha, there were always many things. She wrote poetry and designed clothes. And along with all her talents, she was blessed with beauty.

At 17, Samantha was named Miss San Fernando Valley. That started her on yet another avenue, a modeling career that included spreads in several teen magazines. It was her modeling, however, that started her on a road to the self-destruction of anorexia.

MARGE HEARN
That's when the worry about her weight began. But I think her troubles really started when Gary died. They were very close and she couldn't handle it. She kept getting thinner and thinner.

————

When Chick signed to do *Bowling for Dollars*, he arranged for Samantha to work on the show as a producer with the hope that it would help ease her away from her deep grief over her brother's death.

MARGE HEARN
Sammy had her own office for *Bowling for Dollars*, and she did great. They would do five shows in one day and she had to get enough people for each show, but she did an absolutely wonderful job. And when the people would arrive, Sammy would be the one to come down and greet them.

SHANNON HEARN-NEWMAN
Samantha was such a giving person that she used to go down to skid row with dinners for the homeless.

But despite all her activities, Samantha sunk deeper into an anorexic state.

SHANNON HEARN-NEWMAN

Samantha was like a sister to me. I could say anything to her.

My grandparents would send us out to dinner every night because they knew she liked my company and they hoped she would eat. But she would just move her food around the plate and worry more if I was eating. Which was never a problem for me.

We were always out to dinner, went places like Hawaii and Palm Springs. We went on these trips because my grandparents wanted me to be some sort of influence over Samantha.

But when I would try to talk to her, Samantha would tell me my grandparents had brainwashed me and I was wrong like they were. We were all wrong, all crazy. She wouldn't listen to reason, even from me.

It is a very helpless feeling. Frustrating. And you get mad. I was so mad at her for allowing herself to do this and doing it to everyone around her.

She and I would get in these huge arguments. We'd yell and scream at each other toward the end. I would say, "What the hell are you doing? You are ruining everybody's life around you. Not just yours. You want to kill yourself? Fine. But what about everybody around you?"

My grandmother would be angry one day, but the next, she wanted to do everything for Samantha to make her life comfortable. She wanted Samantha to know she loved her.

MARGE HEARN

We worked so hard trying to get her better. We tried everything. We got her into a self-help group, but she wouldn't stay. She felt degraded. She had lost her self-esteem.

When she wouldn't go to the meetings, Fran and I went anyway to learn all we could about the disease. Anything that could help us help her.

We tried everything. We really tried. But when that thing [anorexia] gets a hold of you, it's tough.

When Samantha learned of a clinic in Switzerland whose operators claimed that they could rejuvenate her body, she asked her mother to take her.

Marge was in no shape to go anywhere. While walking her dogs in her Encino neighborhood, she had been attacked by a larger dog trying to get at her smaller pets. Marge was thrown to the sidewalk, breaking bones in her face and shoulder.

Nevertheless, she packed a bag and headed to Switzerland with Samantha.

MARGE HEARN

That was a tough trip.

And, unfortunately, it was fruitless. By 1990, Samantha's condition had deteriorated so badly that she contracted pneumonia.

She was supposed to go into the hospital on a Saturday. But it wasn't just any Saturday. It was Kentucky Derby Saturday, the day of one of her favorite family activities. Each year, Samantha would write numbers on slips of paper for a drawing. Each number would represent a post position. The family member drawing that number would have the horse in that position.

Samantha got in one last derby drawing before going into the hospital.

Chick and Marge would never again be able to watch the Kentucky Derby without thinking of those slips of paper so meticulously prepared by their daughter.

The day Samantha went into the hospital, the Lakers were scheduled to face Phoenix in a playoff game at the Forum. Chick's streak was well over

113

two thousand straight games at that point, but for once, it seemed meaningless to him.

"I shouldn't go tonight," he told Marge.

"You may as well," she said. "There's nothing you can do at the hospital."

The Lakers' season ended at the Forum, on May 15, 1990, in a 106–103 loss to the Suns.

On May 24, Samantha Janis Hearn died of pneumonia, a complication of anorexia, at 43.

SUSAN STRATTON
Hearn's Producer and Director for a Quarter of a Century

Samantha and I used to talk on the phone all the time. She was so funny. She was smart, really smart. What a horrible nightmare to have happen.

Because Chick and Marge had this terrific marriage, I think they were able to withstand something—losing both of their children—that would have destroyed other people.

SHANNON HEARN-NEWMAN

My grandparents did everything they could with both their children, but they absolutely felt as if they had failed because you always think there is more that you can do. If there had been the help then with drugs and anorexia that there is now, it might have been different.

When my dad passed away, my grandparents were of a generation that didn't talk much about stuff like that. As a couple, they didn't talk to me about it at all. Part of it was my age. And part of it was my grandpa. He would become so emotional when people talked about my dad. It was just so devastating. My grandmother and I would talk about my dad on a very limited basis when my grandpa wasn't around.

But at least when Samantha passed away, we were able to talk more about it. I don't know if it was my age or we had simply all come that much further. We were, unfortunately, all too familiar with that kind of thing.

My grandparents changed some when my dad died, but there was still Samantha, and I was still very young. When Samantha died, and they had lost both of them, that was the end of everything. They didn't even put up a Christmas tree. Everything stopped for them.

I'd say to them, "Why don't you put up a Christmas tree? There has got to be something."

It wasn't until [Shannon's daughter] Kayla came along [in 1995] that they finally came out of it and got a Christmas tree.

CHICK

Sure, we wondered, where did we go wrong? Did we make a mistake? We thought we were doing everything we could. God knows we tried everything. And it ended in death, a double loss for us. You never think about your children dying before you.

We moved out of our house after Gary's death.

We were trying to get away, but grief is something you can never get away from.

For a long time after Gary's death, I would be sitting up there at the Forum thinking that Gary was going to run up, as he always used to, and say, "Hi, Dad."

MARGE HEARN

I couldn't even go to weddings for a long time and watch other girls get married. I got over that. You have to move on. But you never get over the grief.

There isn't a day that goes by that I don't think about them. I'll hear a song they liked or see somebody doing something they liked to do. We were always a close family. We went to all their activities when they were growing up, from swimming to basketball to modeling. We were there with them and for them all of their lives.

I'm always talking about them. I feel like I'm keeping them alive that way.

———

Chick rarely mentioned his kids' names until, at Marge's urging, he consented to discuss them in a story for the *Los Angeles Times* in 2000.

Chick resisted when I first arrived at his house to do that story, but once he started talking about Gary and Samantha, he couldn't stop, the words flowing with the tears.

And after that, for the remainder of his days, he spoke freely of them, bragging about them and their accomplishments to anyone who was interested.

Marge's living room and den are a living memorial to Chick, with his various awards, signed basketballs, photos, and the flag that flew over the nation's capital after his death prominently displayed.

But also precious to Marge is the framed poem on the wall, written to her by Samantha:

> It's no wonder I love you the way you are,
> You're more than a million times above par.
> What can I say that I haven't before?
> You are the best mom and a whole lot more.
> But in the mornings, when you are always going,
> you bug me so much, I'd like to be throwing.
> However at night, it's no wonder you're tired.
> I always annoy you cause that's when I'm wired.
> So what if our lifestyles are not in key?
> I'm so proud that you're the mother of me.
> If you knew how much about you that I brag,
> I'm sure that you would have to join S.A.G.
> I've never known anyone that is so giving,
> and also taught me so much about living.
> I can't believe that you can take so much,
> and handle it all with a loving touch.
> If you ever wonder whom I look up to,

just look in the mirror and you can see who.
I'm thinking of you now although you're in Philly.
You're the greatest mother and a hell of a dilly.

—Samantha J. Hearn

T. J. SIMERS
Los Angeles Times Columnist

I would always go up to sit with Chick and talk about kids before a game. He would want to know about my daughters and I got to know about his children.

One night we got to talking about championship rings. At that point, he had seven. I wanted to know how he determined which one he wore. He told me he had a box at home. He would reach in and pick one out blind. It was a mystery every night which one he would wear.

But he also had a second box in which he kept the ring that he would never wear. That was the one from the 1971–1972 championship, which he had given his son shortly after the Lakers won that title and just before Gary died.

"Because Gary has worn it," he told me, "I can't wear it."

He didn't even want to touch it. So it forever sits in a separate box.

~10 ~
His Broadcast Family:
The Analysts

Al Michaels was stunned, nervous, and a little perplexed.

Here he was, a 21-year-old graduate of Arizona State with dreams of becoming a baseball announcer. Unable to fulfill those dreams, he had returned to Los Angeles—where he had attended Hamilton High School—and taken a job selecting contestants for two television shows, *The Dating Game* and *The Newlywed Game.*

From there, Michaels had moved back into sports by accepting a position in public relations with Jack Kent Cooke's California Sports organization—with the assurance that it might lead to the analyst job with the Kings, just coming into existence for that 1967–1968 season.

That never happened. Instead, Michaels found himself working on the Kings' media guide and chauffeuring coach Red Kelly around to speaking engagements, while keeping his dream alive by spending his nights writing to baseball teams around the country.

But now, here Michaels was on the phone, listening to the booming, authoritative voice of Cooke on the other end.

"Alan," said Cooke in his regal manner, "I want you to get on a plane and go to Salt Lake City. You are going to be Chick Hearn's color announcer on Laker games."

Al Michaels
Laker Broadcast Analyst

I'm thinking, "What??? I'm going to be the Laker color announcer?" Chick had never had a color announcer, and I had no experience with pro basketball. But I certainly wasn't going to mention that to Cooke.

It was the fall of 1967, and the Lakers were still in the preseason. I flew to Salt Lake City, and, I have to say, the reaction I got from Chick was not the warmest. This was obviously not his idea.

Bob Speck
Sports Producer

The ARCO oil company had signed a deal with Cooke for $10 million for five years. But one of the stipulations of the agreement was that there would be a second announcer.

Al Michaels

As it turned out, what I did were halftime scores and maybe a promotion announcement or two. I never did any real analysis for that first game against the Baltimore Bullets or any of the games that followed. It just kind of turned out that way. I figured Chick was just breaking me in a little slowly.

I didn't ask for a job description when I talked to Cooke. Nor was there any discussion of increasing my salary, which was around $250 to $300 a week. I didn't want to broach that subject. All I wanted to do was to get started in the business, get my foot in the door. I didn't want to blow my big chance.

I had never traveled with a sports team, and here I was with the Lakers. I remember that after that first game we flew to Boise, Idaho, slept there, then took a bus the next day to Rupert, Idaho, for another game. I did the same thing on the air. Still no analysis.

Next, we flew to Seattle for a televised game. This time, I did nothing on the air.

That was the pattern. Do some stats, some scores, read a promo, but nothing on television. Yet Chick would always tell the audience, "This is Chick Hearn along with Alan Michaels." I was rolling with the punches, just happy to be there.

BOB SPECK

When Chick raised his left hand, Al was to talk. When he saw Chick's right fist go up, he was to stop. But Chick never raised that left hand, never let him speak. He only let him read halftime scores. I felt so sorry for Al.

AL MICHAELS

The regular season started and nothing changed.

Then, a few games into the season, we were to leave on a two-game trip, starting in Boston. Since I was also the traveling secretary, I had to be at the airport early to hand out the tickets. Remember, those were the days before charter flights.

I left my car at the California Sports offices, which were at Manchester and LaBrea, got to LAX, checked my bag, and started handing out the tickets as the guys came through.

All of sudden, here comes Bill van Breda Kolff, the coach. "I don't know what's going on," he told me, "but I'll take the tickets. Go back to Mr. Cooke's office and see Alan Rothenberg."

I knew Rothenberg was Cooke's hatchet man.

My heart was pounding furiously. I was embarrassed as hell. I had probably lost my job. How was I going to get my car? How was I going to get my bag?

I stood there for 45 minutes until my bag finally came off just as the plane carrying the Lakers was leaving.

"This was just something that didn't work out," Rothenberg told me. "It's the best thing for you."

I had lasted four preseason and seven regular-season games, five of which were televised, which meant I didn't do anything on those.

Later, I finally got an audience with Cooke, who told me, "You'll thank me for this later."

"I'll tell you something, Mr. Cooke," I replied, "I will never thank you for this."

Years later, when I was announcing the Super Bowl that was won by Cooke's Washington Redskins, he told the media he was instrumental in my success.

Four months after my firing, the only time in my life I have ever been fired, I got a job doing play-by-play for the Hawaii Islanders of the Pacific Coast League. From there, I went to the Cincinnati Reds, the San Francisco Giants, and then to ABC.

Looking back, it was clear that Cooke wanted Chick to work with a real color man. I was the sacrificial lamb, the one who greased the skids. Chick's reaction, as Cooke expected, was, "What's this kid doing here?" Then, when Rod Hundley stepped in, Chick was more amenable to having an analyst because at least it was a former player.

I never took it personally. It was all about Cooke and Rothenberg and had very little to do with Chick. If somebody had done to me what they did to him—forcing him into a situation that was sort of ridiculous—I might have acted even worse.

In later years Chick told me how proud he was of what I had accomplished and he was so sincere about it. He said he never missed *Monday Night Football*, and several times after that, he asked me to introduce him at affairs. That was a great thrill.

Now, I'll be doing the NBA Finals this season. It only took me 36 years to get here.

Bob Speck

After Michaels was let go, Cooke was told that Chick didn't want a color man. Cooke called Chick in and said that he couldn't believe that was true.

"I might have had some concerns," Chick told Cooke, "but I welcome a second announcer. That takes some of the load off me."

Chick accepted it, and that was that.

————

But not right away. Not until Hearn went through a few months with Dick Schaad, another analyst who wound up merely reading stats and scores. Then came Hundley.

"HOT" ROD HUNDLEY
Former Laker Player and Broadcast Analyst

Chick was very hard to work with the first year because he didn't want me there. He didn't hire me. The Lakers hired me. He had nothing to do with it. By the second year, he accepted me. Yes, he would rather have worked by himself. Now that I do play-by-play for the Utah Jazz, I have to say I would rather work by myself, too.

I was with the Converse shoe company and had been out of the game for five years when the Lakers offered me the job as Chick's analyst. They paid me $15,000 for the season. In six years as a player with the team, the most I had ever made was $11,500.

When I first started, I had no broadcasting experience. Chick told me, "When I hold my fist up, you've got to cut what you're saying short. If I shake my fist, get out of there now. If you are talking through the free throws and then they put the ball back into play and you're still talking about the last play, I'm going to cut you off."

Sure enough, if I got caught in the middle of a play, he would just step in. I learned how to say something and not take all day to say it. You have to get in and get out instead of lollygagging around. I also learned from Chick that, if you're going to say something as an analyst, it had better be something worth putting on the air. Why just repeat something the play-by-play announcer already said?

I think he was the best basketball announcer ever. I have the ultimate admiration for the man. I learned more sitting there listening to Chick than I could have learned in a hundred years from someone else. I went to the Chick Hearn School of Broadcasting. He showed me how to do play-by-play with enthusiasm, always keeping the listener aware of where the ball was at all times.

He also taught me about simulcasts. Chick would point out, "If you say, referring to a replay, 'Let's take a look at that guy driving down the lane,' how is the guy driving down the street going to look at that? You can never favor television over radio." Chick was a maestro when it came to balancing the two.

If we came back from a commercial late on radio, it didn't matter. Chick would pick it up like it had just started, but he'd do it quickly so he could catch up. He'd remember everything that had happened and work it into the play-by-play.

Chick could get away with some things on radio, too. I remember one time, he called a foul on Jerry West, when it was actually on Elgin Baylor. Chick had made a mistake, but he quickly recovered. He said, "Wait a minute. They changed the call. They gave it to Baylor, not West." I'd be smiling. It was a smart thing to do with a radio audience.

We had a lot of fun together. Chick once said to me, "Rod, Jerry is five for 10 shooting. What's his percentage?"

"Just a minute, Chickie baby," I told him, "I'll look it up."

We didn't always agree on the air. Chick used to say that Billy Hewitt was another Elgin Baylor, but that's because Hewitt had been a number one pick.

I said, on the air, "You tell Mr. Cooke that Billy Hewitt is not going to be another Elgin Baylor."

After I had gotten the play-by-play job in Utah, Chick said to me, "I hear you've been stealing some of my lines."

I said, "Not some of them. All of them."

You just started doing it automatically after you listened to him for so long. He used to call a line-drive shot a "frozen rope." One time, he said, "That was such a frozen rope, you could hang your wash on it."

I just loved the man.

Roy Firestone
National Sportscaster Who also Did a Laker Pregame Show from 1985–1991

Chick loved all his color men off the mike, but once the light went on, he could freeze them out, forget they existed. He could have borderline disdain for anybody who dared to take away from his air time, because he was so immersed in what he was doing.

They were sidekicks as much as analysts, additional characters for Hearn to play off in what was as much a show as a sportscast.

Chick did an All-Star Game with Johnny Most, the Boston announcer. They were two real characters and it's the only time I ever saw Chick really enjoy sharing the microphone.

Lynn Shackelford
Former Laker Broadcast Analyst

Chick and I got along a lot better off the air than on the air.

I played at UCLA and had been on the *John Wooden Show*. Bob Speck saw me and recommended me to Jack Kent Cooke, who, in the job interview, referred to Chick and asked me, "Are you afraid of this man?"

For an audition, I went into a room with Chick and he rattled some play-by-play off the top of his head. I was amazed this guy could sit down in a room and do play-by-play like that. It was my first experience with his talent.

I got hired even though I was only 22 and had no experience. But I knew something about basketball, I had some name value coming out of UCLA, and I was willing to sell season tickets in the off-season over the phone.

Fred Schaus, then the general manager, offered me $12,500 for the year and told me that, if things worked out, he would bump it up to $15,000. When the time came, he only increased me to $14,000. I took it, making the first mistake of my adult life. When I left after seven years, I was only making $19,000.

It was all new to me. Just watching Kareem and Wilt play up close was one of the most exciting things I had ever seen on a basketball court.

Chick really made the game come alive.

He embellished it to make it better than it really was. He needed to do that to sell the game.

When I started, Chick told me, "Objectivity is our primary goal."

I told him, "You'll have no problem with me. I'm just a basketball fan. I don't care who wins."

Chick was riding a big wave, and you just went along with it. You didn't go against it. You didn't criticize what he said on the air.

Cooke thought it would be great to have someone dispute Chick, great to have a debate. Cooke said he thought it would be good for the viewers.

Maybe so, but I didn't think it would be good for the health of our broadcast relationship. Besides, like every great salesman, Chick had a way of convincing you that what he said was right. And if you didn't think so, maybe you weren't looking at it right. So our relationship on the air never developed into what Cooke wanted, and I'm glad. That was not my personality, and it was not Chick's.

The least appealing part of the job was selling those season tickets over the phone. I was making commission on them, but it was awful. Sometimes, when Rod Hundley was supposed to be doing it, he would fail to show up, but would call a secretary and tell her to turn on the light in his office so Cooke would think he was there.

The best part of the job was just listening to Chick. Some of the stuff he said was unbelievable. Kermit Washington once knocked down John Shumate, causing Chick to say, "Mark my words, he's going to hurt somebody some day." And, of course, Washington eventually did, with the punch that severely hurt Rudy Tomjanovich. It was amazing how many of Chick's prognostications were right on.

Nobody on radio could paint a picture like Chick. Not Johnny Most, nor Bill King. None of them.

I finally left because my role wasn't going to change and I wanted to broaden my experience. I had had such great training under Chick that I felt, after seven years, I could work with anyone. I went to Channel 9 and also worked for CBS, NBC, ESPN, and the old Prime Ticket, doing everything from college basketball to beach volleyball.

One thing I wasn't crazy about was that when they hired Riley, they immediately started him at $21,000.

———

Retirement from life as an NBA player didn't go well for Pat Riley. The son of Lee Riley, a minor league manager, Pat was a basketball star at the University of Kentucky, a first-round draft choice of the then–San Diego Rockets, and a nine-year NBA veteran, including five seasons with the Lakers. Riley was forced into early retirement, leaving the Phoenix Suns at 31 because of a bad knee.

PAT RILEY
Former Laker Player, Broadcast Analyst, Assistant Coach, and Coach
I was actually thinking of going into the shoe business.

———

That didn't work out. Neither did several attempts to get into college coaching.

Instead, Riley hung out at the beach, played volleyball, wrote down his sometimes bitter observations about the afterlife of an NBA player, and took out his frustrations on his home, tearing down walls and ceilings in a master remodeling project while what he really wanted to do was tear down the barriers that had sprung up between him and his sport.

The low point came the night Riley went to the Forum to see his old team play. He didn't want to bother the players in the locker room afterward, but he figured they'd renew acquaintances in the press lounge, the hot social spot after games.

Not for Riley.

The usher guarding the door refused him entrance. Riley flashed the championship ring he had won with the 1971–1972 Lakers.

Sorry, he was told, ex-players are not allowed.

And then, when he least expected it, that press door swung open after Lynn Shackelford left Hearn's side.

PAT RILEY

I got a phone call from Chick. He knew I was doing nothing and wanted to know if I wanted to become his analyst.

I felt I could work with Chick. I had great respect for him. Chick was hyper, energetic when he got into a game. He didn't have time for an upstart. You just had to toe the line and keep up with him. If you weren't prepared, you could be lost, embarrassed.

But I found my niche. He would challenge me to make three or four good points. He would encourage me to do the *New York Times* crossword puzzle because, he said, it would be great for my vocabulary.

Chick would tell me when he thought I was good. Some of the half-time pieces I did he thought were really good—pieces I did on Magic [Johnson], Norm [Nixon], and [Spencer] Haywood, with music I added. I thought Chick was a very nurturing man.

We didn't get into disputes on the air because I would not disagree with him. If you did, you would lose. He had a very singular voice, made very cogent points. Trying to create opinions that went against his opinions was not a winning strategy.

SUSAN STRATTON
Hearn's Producer and Director for a Quarter of a Century

We always used to tease Chick that he didn't really want a color announcer, but I don't know that that's right. I think he just didn't want to have to talk to them about their shortcomings.

It took me forever to realize this, but if you did something that bothered him, whatever it was, he had trouble saying to you, "I wish you wouldn't do that. When that ball reaches this point on the court, I need you to stop talking."

It was just something that was really hard for him to do. So, he needed to have somebody else say it for him.

128

Pat Riley

He was a very, very bright man who could express himself very well. And he was very honest. If it was a boring game, a dull game, he would let people know that in his enthusiastic way.

And he was funny. He used to kid me about my voice. I didn't have a very good one. It was nasal because I had broken [my nose] a couple of times. Chick would hold his own nose between his fingers and say, "Hey, Riley," mimicking me.

We really liked each other. We were both Irish, had the same birthday, and had a real good relationship as men.

Susan Stratton

Pat owes his career to Chick. Of the color announcers I worked with—Pat, Keith Erickson, and Stu Lantz—Pat was probably the one that had the hardest time, because he wasn't as verbal as the other two.

We were doing a pregame show in Milwaukee. Chick and Pat were on the floor and they had a color drawing of the Bradley Center, which was being built at the time. The floor design was revolutionary for that era.

There was only one mike because Chick didn't want his color announcer to have his own microphone. That arrangement went on for a number of years.

Chick told the audience, "There's going to be this new arena," and, instead of handing the mike to Pat while he held up the drawing, Chick put the mike under his left arm. So, of course, you couldn't hear what he was saying.

But Pat was not going to get that mike.

The broadcast position in Milwaukee was way up in the crowd. I told Chick, "You have to go back up there so you can open the game. We'll leave Pat to close out the pregame show."

Pat, new at the time, had to fill a minute. He looked in the camera and said, "Welcome back. The Lakers are getting ready to play the Milwaukee Bucks and Chick and I will be with you in just a few minutes. Good-bye, everybody."

And that was it. No, Pat, no!

He told me later, "I couldn't think of anything to say."

KEITH ERICKSON
Former Laker Broadcast Analyst

When I retired from playing, I got hired by CBS. Sitting there with a headset on frightened me to death. But I felt comfortable with Chick.

My wife, Adrienne, and I had been friends with Chick and Marge since the days when I played for the Lakers. He asked me to come on as a temporary analyst while Riley went down to become Paul Westhead's assistant. The idea was, once Riley returned to the booth, I would be out of there.

I went into it with my eyes wide open, knowing this was Chick's baby, Chick's show. Any idiot knew that. That was the way it was going to be. I would talk only when he needed to take a breath. I certainly wasn't going to try to force my will on him. If there was an opportunity, I would speak, but it wasn't my intent to get my opinion heard. My intent was to complement Chick. I would have loved to have expressed more of an opinion, but the rules were what they were and you don't bring your own rules into that situation.

One time, though, I did do something extra on my own that Chick didn't even know about. We were in San Antonio eating dinner at the arena before a game when I saw one of those Miss Bud Lite girls. A very large girl, if you know what I mean.

I told her we were doing a broadcast back to L.A. and asked her if she wanted to have a little fun. She was agreeable.

The broadcast was to open with Chick and me on the floor of the arena. I had the girl standing off to one side. The red light came on and Chick said, "Hello, everybody, I'm Chick Hearn along with Keith Erickson from San Antonio, Texas, where tonight . . ."

At that moment, the girl came on camera, ran up to Chick, and gave him a big hug and kiss. Chick, completely caught off guard, looked at me on camera and said, "Where are we?"

That moment was the best, although our producer, Susan Stratton, wasn't too happy about it.

Chick could usually handle any situation. One night, the Lakers were playing the Cleveland Cavaliers in Richfield, Ohio. There was a horrible storm, it was freezing cold, and our bus to the game was inching along on icy roads. When we got there, there was no heat in the arena, no food, the coffee was cold, everything was wrong. And Chick was complaining about all of it right up until it was time to go on the air.

But once the camera went on, Chick broke into a big smile and said, "Hello, everybody, this is Chick Hearn along with Keith Erickson from Richfield, Ohio, where tonight, the Lakers will play the Cleveland Cavaliers. And what a game we are going to have for you."

It was like he was doing the NBA Finals from Malibu. He had not had one good thing to say for three hours, but once we went on the air, he was on his game, no less than any game he had ever done. He was a great pro to work alongside. He was always prepared when the light went on.

He was a real legend.

Susan Stratton

Calvin Murphy, who used to play with the Rockets, had this drum corps playing at halftime one time in Houston. We had this little feature interview, commercials, and then we were going to come back live to the announcers.

Keith, meanwhile, went off to the locker room. We did the interview, did the commercials, and this band is still on the floor. It was one of the longest halftimes in the history of the NBA. It went on for 44 minutes.

Chick was out there holding the fort while Keith had disappeared. We couldn't find him. I sent someone in search of him and we finally located him just before halftime ended.

I said to Keith, "Where in the hell were you?"

He said, "I didn't think you could be on the air with that band."

I said, "Keith, we were live, *OK*?"

STU LANTZ
Laker Broadcast Analyst

It was a real pleasure to be around Chick all of those years.

After retiring from the NBA, I worked for CBS and then the Clippers, while they were still in San Diego, before joining Chick.

It was certainly different working with him. I would start talking and he would start talking. There was a lot of stepping on toes between Chick and me in the beginning. It was almost as if he wasn't hearing what I was saying. He would take a breath as long as he needed to take a breath. Then, he would just start talking and keep going. If I still had, like, half a sentence to get out, we'd talk together. He had no patience. None whatsoever. He got mad. But it was typical of two people learning one another.

There was always the thought that he would cut me off. That window could shut real quick. Whatever you had in your thought process, you had to get it out there really, really fast.

Later on in our togetherness, he would apologize for cutting me off. That's when I knew there was progress being made. He would say, "Excuse me, Stu."

We did a lot of bantering on the air. People thought we were arguing, but we weren't. We were just showing differences of opinion. He didn't take it too well at first.

I would say, "No, that wasn't a bad call. This is what happened." Then he would come up with some way of defending his point, I would defend my point, and we would have these debates.

Sometimes play would resume and he would have to end our discussion. When the next break came, if he was quiet, then you knew you had perturbed him. He was not real happy.

But I was going to do the thing I do. I wasn't going to try to do what they did in the past. I knew it was going to be a different scenario because I was obviously different than anyone Chick had worked with before.

As the years went on, I think he started to understand how good it was that somebody had a different opinion than his, that you didn't have to agree with everything he said.

But I give credit to Chick because it was Chick who made the adjustment in allowing me to do things. It was him. I didn't change. He was the one who made it easy for me.

Susan Stratton

We were in Hawaii for the preseason and I wanted Chick and Stu to do something different, something fun.

So I decided we would mike them and take them out in this outrigger, Captain Coco's boat. Chick didn't want to do it and Stu is not a great swimmer. But I told Jerry West about it and he thought it was hysterical. So now Chick and Stu are kind of forced into it.

We did this piece with them in the outrigger that is just priceless. It is so funny. We replayed it to death because I could never get them back in that outrigger again.

Stu Lantz

Chick was still very sharp as he got older. I thought any mistakes he made were not unlike something I would do at times. I would forget a name and he would help me. But nobody ever looked at it that way. They didn't make a big deal out of him helping me, but I got a lot of mail about helping him.

~ 11 ~
His Broadcast Family:
The Crew

A junior staff producer and director at Channel 9 in L.A. who had been cat-apulted into one of the most prestigious sports jobs in all of television, Susan Stratton found herself talking into a headset to one of the biggest names in sportscasting. What more could she ask for?

Well, it would have been nice if that big name had, in turn, talked to her.

For the first two months of the 1976–1977 season, Stratton's first as pro-ducer and director of Laker telecasts, Chick Hearn wouldn't speak to her.

SUSAN STRATTON
Hearn's Producer and Director for a Quarter of a Century

This was the seventies. There were no women doing this. The idea of a station naming a woman to do this job was a revolutionary move. Chick was an old-school man who didn't think a woman could handle it. That's what I think it basically boiled down to.

———

Stratton wouldn't have even gotten the opportunity to break down the gender barrier keeping her outside the TV truck had it not been for Jack Kent Cooke, whose Lakers and Kings had been on Channel 5.

They shared that broadcast outlet with the Angels. In the spring of 1976 the Kings were in the playoffs and the Angels were in spring training. Channel 5 officials announced they would preempt hockey for baseball.

Cooke said that was ridiculous; postseason play was far more important than preseason exhibition games. A reasonable argument except for the fact that hockey ratings weren't even on the same radar screen as those of baseball.

And even more importantly, the Angels were owned by Gene Autry. As was Channel 5. End of argument.

But arguments with Jack Kent Cooke ended only after he had made his point. He had been in a similar situation a decade earlier. When he bought the Lakers and attempted to negotiate a new contract with Sports Arena officials, he was told he was stuck with the deal they had negotiated with the previous owner, Bob Short.

Cooke threatened to pull his team out and build his own arena. Sports Arena officials laughed at him. Cooke later said that if they had only laughed, he would have laughed with them, but one of the officials, according to Cooke, actually said, "Ha, ha, ha."

Infuriated, Cooke said good-bye, found land in a neighboring city named Inglewood, and built the Forum.

This time, it was nothing quite as dramatic. He told Channel 5 officials that, if they didn't run his hockey telecasts, he'd move to another station. Nobody is known to have said, "ha, ha, ha," but they also didn't budge. The Angels played on.

And Cooke moved on, to Channel 9.

Stratton had been schooled in basketball by her parents. Both had played the sport. Stratton played for her high school in Auburn, outside Philadelphia, where her father was principal and basketball coach.

As an adult, she had settled into a satisfying job producing and directing in Washington, D.C., including some work on Redskin telecasts. Stratton came west, reluctantly, when her husband got a job at KTTV in Los Angeles.

Hired by Channel 9, she got the opportunity to get into her first love, sports, when a position on Rams telecasts opened up.

SUSAN STRATTON

All the senior staff members wanted to do entertainment. It was a big break for me. Really big.

She became producer/director of Rams coach Chuck Knox's show.

With the arrival of the Lakers, Stratton sailed into waters uncharted for a woman.

SUSAN STRATTON

Channel 9 began its association with Jack Kent Cooke by doing 25 Laker games and 20 Kings games.

Chick and I started that season pretty rocky, a bloody brawl. Not fun. It was two months before he would talk to me. I had to go through intermediaries.

At least Jerry West, who was then the coach, would talk to me. He got me on the team bus, which was, again, unheard of for a woman. That was a breakthrough.

Then came the breakthrough with Hearn.

SUSAN STRATTON

We had a game in Piscataway, New Jersey, with the Nets. They were using this school facility.

I got there early because I was brand new. I went in and looked at the game site, a gymnasium, and found out really quickly that it was a disaster. The college team was practicing until 6:30 at night. Our game was at 7:30. We were not going to be allowed into the building to do anything until the college players were done. The camera positions were

Chick

nonexistent. In the only place we could have put cameras, there was a glass partition with etchings on the glass.

If setup time for a show is not there, you'll suffer for it. It's the same thing with camera angles. They are your lifeblood. They have to be correct. And when they're not, it shows. I called the station, talked to the general manager, Lionel Schaen, and told him, "This is really bad."

He said, "What do you think we should do?"

I said, "I don't see that we are going to be able to do this show. I think we ought to cancel it." I told the Lakers the same thing.

But the Lakers and the station decided they would go ahead with the telecast because it was on the schedule and the commercial advertising had already been sold.

Chick called and actually talked to me for once, saying, "I understand you think there's a problem here."

I told Chick the same thing I had told the others.

"I'm sure it's not as bad as that," he told me.

That really ticked me off. "I'll do everything I can to make it work out," I promised him.

We did the game and it really was a nightmare. What I told them was wrong *was* wrong.

At first, I didn't understand the significance of that night for me. I thought it would be my fault because I couldn't stop this disaster. They think I'm terrible, I thought, and this will be the crowning blow. I really didn't get it.

It turned out to be the other way around because I had warned them. It broke the ice for me. I found out just how monumental that game was for me the next day when Mr. Cooke himself had a call put through to me.

"Hello, Mrs. Stratton, this is Rosemary Garmand for Mr. Cooke. Are you available to take a call?" the voice on the other end said.

"Yes!!!"

Mr. Cooke got on the line. "Mrs. Stratton"—I remember this word for word—"I want you to know we are absolutely delighted with the job

138

you are doing for us," he said, "and we hope our association with you will continue for a long time. And I wanted to tell you that personally."

I called Lionel all excited and said, "Do you know what just happened? Mr. Cooke called me!"

After that, Chick and I started talking a little bit. I was trying as hard as I could to forge a relationship with him because I knew that it was something I needed to do. I tried to think of things I could do to help him.

He was a very precise man, very orderly. There were things I did with his broadcast position to make his work easier for him. When he would come to the building, things were finally the way he wanted them. Someone was trying to help him. When he saw that, he responded to it.

Chick didn't have a mean bone in his body.

I was pretty careful because I didn't want to step on his toes. And that went on for maybe a year. I would suggest things, like peripheral production matters. But then, as we got to know each other better, it kind of grew from that.

KEITH ERICKSON
Former Laker Broadcast Analyst

Susan was terrific, the best thing that ever happened to Chick. She did what she could to make his job easier. She would take the brunt of whatever was going on.

He ended up adoring her. He had tremendous respect for her, great admiration.

SUSAN STRATTON

His support for me meant everything. I'll never forget it—I can't even talk about it without getting choked up.

Remember, I was a woman in a position where there weren't any other women. Chick was crucial to the fact that I have a career. If Chick Hearn said she's OK, then she must be OK.

He taught me a lot of interesting things about television. He taught me not to be boring. That's the kiss of death.

And he certainly wasn't.

He taught me to be disciplined. I try to do that today. He never gave up. No one was as demanding as he was.

That man had a mind like a steel trap. He could remember numbers. He could look at a box score, you could take it away from him, and he could still remember what that box score was. When we would sit together on the bus, I would take it away, and he could still remember what a guy's field-goal percentage was and that a guy was 10 for 22 from the field.

————

Hearn could infuriate Stratton, never more so than when he would promise the audience a replay Stratton couldn't come up with.

Susan Stratton

Chick would say, "Susan, let's look at that replay."

Uh, no, we won't.

At first I would get mad when he did that. Sometimes things go wrong. When you go to look at a replay, it may not all be there. Maybe the feet aren't right or maybe the hands aren't right or something's not quite right about the angle. We have to go to it so quickly that often, we don't have the time to really check it to make sure we have it all perfectly.

Chick would say, "Well, that replay doesn't really show what we're trying to tell you. Our producer/director tonight is Sue Stratton. And she and her crew are doing a fine job."

"Chick," I would tell him, "first you criticize the replay and then you say my name."

Most of the time, what he said was nice and complimentary. He always noticed the people around him and said who they were. Chick was very loyal to people he cared about.

_____

One replay proved more memorable than all the others Stratton and Hearn have been involved in over the years, because it actually affected a game.

It was against the Spurs in November 1982, back in the days when they played in San Antonio's HemisFair Arena. Spurs guard Johnny Moore, fouled by Magic Johnson, had connected on two free throws to put his team ahead, 116–113, with only three seconds to play.

Accurate?

Not according to Hearn's monitor. Looking at a replay, the Lakers announcer, sitting courtside, saw Johnson's foul coming with several more seconds remaining.

CHICK

Our coach, Pat Riley, could not convince either referee to give the Lakers more time.

During the timeout that followed, I yelled out to referee Jack Madden, "There's a mistake being made. The clock should have been stopped at either five or six seconds. Do you want to see the monitor?"

When he didn't show any interest, when he didn't even respond to me, I figured he was going to disregard what I had said. But he didn't. He went over to the timekeeper, whose name was Red Shaw. Shaw admitted, "I didn't see the foul called or hear the whistle." He was admitting he had let some seconds get away.

_____

The Lakers got a crucial second added to the clock, and Laker guard Norm Nixon was subsequently fouled, again leaving three seconds to play—but this time it was an undisputed three. Nixon made the first free throw to leave the Lakers two back at 116–114. He faked the second, but pulled the ball back as if it were on a string, causing players from both sides to tumble into the lane. Madden ruled it was a double lane violation and called for a jump ball. Kareem

Abdul-Jabbar won the tip from San Antonio's Artis Gilmore and fed the ball to Johnson, who whipped it to Nixon, who tied up the game at the buzzer with an 18-foot jump shot.

The Lakers went on to win in double overtime, 137–132.

"I'm glad Chick is on our side," Pat Riley, then the Laker coach, said afterward.

Susan Stratton

An announcer getting an official to react to a replay? That would never happen today.

Chick

I felt very proud that Jack listened to me. I think my relationship with the officials was something I earned over the years.

———

Yet that's not the end of the story. That double-overtime victory didn't stand up. Not because of Hearn, but because of Madden's ruling on the double lane violation. Larry O'Brien, then the NBA commissioner, upheld a San Antonio protest, saying a jump ball was the incorrect call. Because Nixon did not let go of the ball, there was no violation and he was required to shoot the free throw again.

Which he did, four and a half months later on the Lakers' next trip to San Antonio. This time, Nixon shot and deliberately missed, but the Spurs gained possession, added a free throw, and won, 117–114.

After the final three seconds had been replayed, the two teams played a regulation game, which San Antonio also won, 114–109. It was the only Laker doubleheader in team history, and they lost both games.

Nevertheless, it would be the replay Hearn and Stratton would never forget.

MITCH CHORTKOFF
Former Laker Beat Writer for the *Santa Monica Outlook*
I'm sitting on a plane near Chick and Susan. A guy comes up the aisle looking as if he's going to ask for an autograph.

He reaches our seat, hands Susan something to sign, and says, "You must be the famous Susan Stratton who Chick is always mad at."

ROY FIRESTONE
National Sportscaster Who also Did a Laker Pregame Show from 1985–1991
When I was doing the Laker pregame show, I'd hear Chick and Susan bickering during commercial breaks, but then they'd hug and make up before the break was over.

———

Stratton wasn't the only one with memories of working with Hearn.

RAY STALLONE
Former Laker Statistician
In the mid-eighties, I was hired to be Chick's statistician in Chicago and Milwaukee. I got the job because I was the sports information director at DePaul.

Of all the announcers I met—Jack Buck, Gary Bender, Doug Collins—no one compared to Chick Hearn in terms of preparation. This guy was so organized and so elaborate. He had these customized charts and colored pens. Because he also did television, he had his hairbrush, his makeup kit, and his mirror. He couldn't just jump out of his seat and go on TV.

You knew not to touch any of his stuff.

I knew I was watching a landmark figure. This was not just a guy who showed up half an hour before the game and asked for a roster.

CURT SANDOVAL
L.A. Sportscaster

A few years ago, the Lakers had a preseason game in Anaheim with a 6:30 start. We were doing a live shot [a segment on Channel 7 news], so I got there at 3:30. As I walked into the Arrowhead Pond, there were maybe three or four media guys hanging around, just shooting the bull.

I heard a voice, looked up, and there was Chick, already at his seat up in the stands. He wasn't talking to anybody. He didn't have time for that. What I had heard was him practicing his play-by-play out loud.

Chick once told me that, the way a player warms up before a game, he would warm up his voice. When he wasn't broadcasting his imaginary game, he was doing his stats, making his charts.

For a broadcast person like myself, what a great lesson to learn: preparation, preparation, preparation. Chick started practicing three hours before the game. There's the oldest guy in the building diligently preparing for a preseason game. We can get so complacent in this business because we think we know what we are doing.

This was a guy who had been doing it forever and he was still the hardest working guy around.

———

Despite all the preparation imaginable, play-by-play announcers are on live, meaning something can, and inevitably does, go wrong.

No problem for Hearn, who was a master at improvising.

SUSAN STRATTON

In Boston Garden, Chick was situated way up on the balcony, so we would put Keith Erickson on the floor for the pregame show and then he would join Chick for the game.

On one occasion, we had this monster show planned, all this stuff.

We went on the air, and Chick, standing up there alone on the balcony, script in hand, began by saying, "Live from Boston Garden."

I looked up at the monitor just in time to see him drop the script, the pages floating down all those levels to the floor.

But as it turned out, Chick did a really great job ad-libbing.

———

Even when the breakdowns were obvious to the audience, Hearn never lost his composure.

One night in Indiana, Hearn told Stratton to get a shot of the writers traveling with the team, all of whom were sitting courtside. Hearn wanted to introduce them to his audience.

Something, however, got lost in the transmission. Because the next thing Hearn saw on his monitor was waiters serving food in a luxury suite.

A lesser wit might have been flustered.

"No," Hearn said without missing a beat, "the guys I want to show serve up a lot of baloney, but they're not waiters."

RAY STALLONE

If he saw something that caught his eye, he would weave that into the broadcast.

One night in Chicago, in the first quarter of a Lakers-Bulls game, a local guy proposed to his girlfriend with a message on the scoreboard, exactly the kind of thing Chick loved.

It had no relevance to the game and you would think people in L.A. couldn't care less.

After the girl said yes, Chick spent the next 10 minutes, through fouls and fast breaks and all the rest, talking about this proposal.

Susan had the cameras continually showing the couple in the stands.

With two minutes to go in the first half, as a camera again zoomed in, the couple had gotten up and was leaving the arena.

Chick, in his inimitable style, said, "I think she told him, 'Let's get out of here and get to that altar before you change your mind.'"

SHERON BELLIO
Producer, Laker Talk Show

He'd say something so brilliant, so quick-witted—remember, the guy was in his eighties—and then he'd turn and nudge me with his big, pointy elbows as if to say, "Wasn't that a good one?"

He was always encouraging me in my career, telling me that, if there was anything he could do, just to let him know.

Just by sitting with Chick, I was somebody important.

BOB SPECK
Sports Producer

They started simulcasts in 1977 to satisfy both the radio and television audiences. Also, Jack Kent Cooke liked the idea of saving money by cutting down on the number of announcers.

RAY STALLONE

I had never seen simulcasts, an announcer doing both radio and TV. I grew up in New York and lived in Chicago. My first experience with simulcasts was when the Lakers came to Chicago. I watched Chick standing on the court, talking into a camera, then coming over to do radio. It was a totally unique experience for me, but he made it seem routine. I think the simulcast is one of the legacies he should be remembered for.

I would call friends in L.A. after a broadcast and ask them about a particular play. Did they listen on the radio, I wanted to know, or see it on TV? Did it seem to them more like a radio call or a TV call?

What was remarkable to me was that people in L.A. didn't have an opinion. That's how good Chick was. The radio call was not so overdone that the television audience felt overwhelmed.

SUSAN STRATTON

When Chick was in his sixties, we wanted to copy the networks, who were using graphics. Graphics are half the show now, but then it was a new technology. A lot of the old-time announcers didn't want to use graphics because they thought that was taking away from them. Some of those old-timers had to be dragged kicking and screaming into this new phase of sports broadcasting.

At first, Chick didn't want to do it either, but then he said, OK, he would try it. He wasn't afraid to attempt something new.

The only thing he insisted on was that when we put an average in for, say, free throws or field-goal percentage, he wanted us to do so down to the decimal point, like 76.1 or 81.6. So that's what we did. He wanted it that way because he liked the option of deciding if he was going to round off, say, 83.6 to 84 or 83. If he thought that player should have a little more, that the numbers didn't seem quite right, he would group to 84.

———

Stratton wasn't the only one whose firm bond with Hearn began on shaky ground.

Lon Rosen
Sports Agent

When I was a 20-year-old intern for the Lakers, I was asked to fill in as Chick's statistician. Again, I was 20, so I was somewhat intimidated by him. But Chick was always very nice. He made sure to say your name so that your mom and dad would hear it, as would all your friends.

But in this one game, I made a mistake. I missed a foul. And for the rest of the game, he would not stop berating me on the air about messing up.

How could a USC student do that, he wanted to know.

I refused to do stats after that for two years because I was afraid of taking the abuse from him.

———

But as was the case with Stratton, Rosen's relationship with Hearn went from fragile to familial.

147

LON ROSEN

When I got married to my wife, Laurie, we invited Chick and Marge. Right before the ceremony started, he pulled me aside and said, "Lonnie, are you sure this is what you want to do? This is a very important decision."

"I know," I said, "but I'm getting married in five minutes."

"I just want to give you one more chance," he insisted. "I'm making sure you want to do this."

RAY STALLONE

He made such an impression on me because he was so remarkable. If you handed him a statistic, like, Magic has 12 assists, he wouldn't use it right away. He would use it when he felt it mattered. So you had to constantly stay on top of your stat-keeping because you never knew when he would use them. If he waited five more minutes, Magic might have five more assists.

Once he used whatever information you gave him, he got rid of it. Some announcers would refer back to something three times. Not Chick. He would use it once and get it out of there.

I always had to be on my toes. I could never look up in the stands for my friends or, heaven forbid, look up at the scoreboard for an out-of-town score.

If I did, I knew what could happen because Chick would not only call the game, but what was going on around him as well. So if I didn't deliver the stats, he would say, "Oh, my guy from DePaul, Ray Stallone, is letting me down."

JOE MCDONNELL
L.A. Talk-Show Host

When the Clippers were still in San Diego, there was a disaster one night with the lines for the broadcast. The phone guy was struggling to fix it, but time was going by.

Chick was getting more and more anxious. "Forget tonight," he said off the air. "Is this guy going to get this thing fixed before the next time we come down here?"

Finally, the repairs were done, everything was running smoothly, and Chick, on the air, said, "We were fortunate to have working with us one of the greatest technicians imaginable. Bless him for the great job he has done."

RAY STALLONE

The first time I met Chick, he asked me my name and where I went to school, and never again did I have to worry about Chick remembering my name, even though I only saw the guy twice a year.

When I got a job with a McDonald's marketing agency in Chicago, Chick would say to me on the air, "Hey, you've got to lower the prices on those hamburgers."

I had lots of friends in L.A. who would tell me, "Chick mentioned you again. Don't get a big head."

No one compared to Chick because he made everyone around him part of his broadcast, from ushers to vendors.

I figured it must be such a joy to listen to him in L.A. because you got all this flavor.

———

For Hearn, there was also the name game: challenging, innovative, and sometimes downright hilarious.

ALISON BOGLI
Laker Media Relations Staff

The first day I ever did the game notes, Chick called in, like he always did, to go over the names on the roster. The Lakers were playing the Portland Trail Blazers. Most of the names were regular names, until I got to Boumtje Boumtje. I told Chick that was the player's name, but he just didn't believe me.

I spelled it out for him, but he said, "Two last names? No, no. What's his number? I'm just going to call him by his number."

RAY STALLONE

Coming from New York, I was used to the Marv Albert call: "Frazier to Reed to DeBusschere."

Chick would use first names instead, or nicknames: "Magic to Kareem to Big Game James." It was so terribly unique.

JOHN IRELAND
L.A. Sportscaster

Toward the end of Chick's career, we were in Vancouver when the Grizzlies still played there, and Snoop Dogg was sitting in the front row across the court from Chick.

The Grizzlies, terrible that year, were being blown out by the Lakers in the fourth quarter. Part of that run was a steal and dunk by Kobe Bryant. As Kobe ran back up court, he went by Snoop Dogg, who stood up to give him a high five. Kobe matched that high five without breaking stride.

We got that on camera, and Sue Stratton decided to use it as a bump shot [a slow-motion shot used when going into or coming out of a station break].

So Sue said into Chick's ear, "Hey, we're going to show you a picture of Kobe with Snoop Dogg."

Chick said, "Who?"

Stu Lantz chimed in, saying, "Come on, Chick, that's Snoop Dogg. You know, Snoop."

Chick, still confused, said, "Dog what?"

A member of our crew asked Chick, "Do you want me to write it down for you? It's Snoop Dogg. He's a rapper. He records CDs."

"What's his name?" asked Chick again.

"Snoop Dogg."

"All right."

We came back on the air, Sue rolled the shot, and Chick said, "Welcome back to Vancouver where Kobe gets some support from *Snoopy*."

~ 12 ~

His Other Jobs

Before the first time he described Elgin Baylor weaving and soaring to the basket, or Jerry West coldly, calmly swishing a jumper at the buzzer, Chick Hearn's voice was familiar to L.A. sports fans.

BOB SPECK
Sports Producer

Chick came out here to do USC football and basketball, and sports on KNX radio. Tom Harmon was originally offered USC, but took UCLA instead.

Chick soon added the TV sportscasts on Channel 4 News. There was a conflict between the radio and television sports reports, which were both on at the same time. Chick didn't want to give either one up, and, though it might be hard to believe nowadays, neither station knew about Chick's other job.

He would tape his radio show at the KNX studio on Sunset and El Centro, and then literally run several blocks to where Channel 4 was located, at Sunset and Vine in those days.

This went on for a few months. Then one day Bill Parry, a sports consultant at KNX, was listening to Chick on his radio station when he flipped on the television, and there was Chick as well.

That was that. Chick gave up the radio job.

———

Whatever he did on the air, Hearn was the consummate entertainer and a master of one-liners who could keep an audience enthralled whether he was broadcasting a game decided on the final shot or a game decided before the final quarter even began, whether he was capturing the color and excitement of a college game or the tension and drama of a championship fight.

When he was posthumously inducted in 2003 into the Basketball Hall of Fame in Springfield, Massachusetts, it was just the last, and he would probably say, the greatest of a long list of honors.

Among his many honors were the 1992 Basketball Hall of Fame Curt Gowdy Media Award; an Emmy award for excellence in basketball coverage; the Academy of Television Arts and Sciences 50th Anniversary Award; a Victor Award for lifetime achievement; and the first-ever Cable Ace Award. He is a member of the American Sportscasters Association Hall of Fame and of both the Southern California Sports Broadcasters Hall of Fame and the Los Angeles Athletic Club Hall of Fame. He was two-time National Sportscaster of the Year; seven-time California Sportscaster of the Year; three-time Golden Mike Award winner; and Cedars-Sinai Journalist of the Year. To top it all off, he has a star on the Hollywood Walk of Fame.

Hearn announced stock car racing from the 87th Street Speedway in Chicago, the first Muhammad Ali–Joe Frazier fight, and basketball at the Olympics in 1992. He did football—both college and pro; University of Nevada sports, Las Vegas, basketball, golf, and tennis; horse racing; and the Rose Bowl parade.

Hearn appeared in 11 movies, from *The Loved One* in 1965 to *Love and Basketball* in 2000. Among his other films were *White Men Can't Jump* and *The Gambler*.

He also appeared in 21 television shows, ranging from *My Three Sons* (1962) to *Police Woman* (1977) to *Matlock* (1987) to *Disneyland* and *The Simpsons* (both 1991). When the Harlem Globetrotters somehow wound up on *Gilligan's Island*, Hearn was there on the beach to broadcast their game.

Of all his appearances away from the hardwood, however, Hearn is best remembered for the classic seventies television show *Bowling for Dollars*.

Bob Speck

John Reynolds, the president and general manager at Channel 5, was looking for a host for *Bowling for Dollars*. He told me he had auditioned all these game-show people but couldn't find anybody who was right.

I had known Chick since he first came to L.A. I was an 18-year-old copy boy in the newsroom at KNX and he would come in at 6:00 A.M. to do sports cut-ins on the old Bob Crane morning show. I used to type up the scores for Chick.

I thought he would be perfect for *Bowling for Dollars*. He had already done something like that starting in the late fifties. It was a game show with Milton Berle in a bowling alley behind CBS called the Hollywood Legion Lanes, so named because it was built on the site of the old Hollywood Legion Stadium. People would bowl with Chick doing the announcing and Berle telling jokes.

Chick was just great with people. And he could be so dramatic. One time a Laker got hurt and Chick told his audience, "I don't want to alarm his family in Los Angeles, but this guy might he dead." It turned out the guy was fine and I think he even played in the second half.

All in all, I thought Chick would be a natural at *Bowling for Dollars*. I told Reynolds, "I got a guy I'd like you to try."

"This is not another one of your damn sports shows," Reynolds told me, throwing in a few expletives. He hated sports because it always seemed to preempt his programming.

But because he didn't have any alternatives, Reynolds took a look at Chick, and told me, "I've decided this guy of yours is pretty good." I knew Reynolds didn't even know who Chick was. I don't think Reynolds ever watched a Laker game.

But he loved Chick on *Bowling for Dollars*, for good reason. The show became very, very successful, number one in its time slot. Reynolds had wanted to start Chick at scale, $250. I insisted on $500, and Chick doubled that in time.

He would come in and do a month of shows in a day and a half, boom, boom, boom. They'd start the tape and wouldn't stop. There was no need to. He knew what he was doing.

———

The show produced some classic Hearn performances still treasured by viewers who wouldn't know basketball from basket weaving.

John Ireland
L.A. Sportscaster

This nice lady, probably in her forties, came on the show. "Let's welcome our next contestant," Chick said. "She's a mother of two and a Cub Scout den mother. She'd like to win money tonight on *Bowling for Dollars* so that she can take her family to Las Vegas."

This woman got up and rolled the ball right into the gutter.

Without missing a beat, Chick said, "If you bowl like that, you ain't even going to make it to Pomona."

Another night on *Bowling for Dollars*, Chick committed the sin every guy fears, and Chick did it live on Channel 5.

"We'd like to introduce our next contestant. Congratulations and welcome to *Bowling for Dollars*," said Chick as a big, big gal came on stage. "When are you due?"

She looked at him angrily and said, "I'm not pregnant."

Chick never blinked, simply saying, "OK, well have at it then."

Jeanie Buss
Laker Executive Vice President of Business Operations

As a kid, *Bowling for Dollars* was one of my favorite shows. It had nothing to do with the fact that it was a game show where people tried to win money. It had to do with the way Chick reacted to the contestants. He was priceless, the look on his face or a simple comment that would some-times go over the contestant's head. We'd be at home just cracking up.

As memorable as Hearn was on *Bowling for Dollars*, he was even better on the Laker pregame talk show he hosted for years. He would be entertaining, witty, and biting when necessary. He would be tough on the Lakers when they deserved it.

And on callers as well.

One night, a caller told Hearn how much he and his 10-year-old son, Johnny, loved Hearn's broadcasts, how they never missed a word he said on the air. It was obvious Hearn was enjoying the praise.

"What can I do for you?" he asked the caller.

"Well, while I love basketball, I would like to propose a couple of rule changes."

"And what would those be?" asked Hearn.

"For one thing, you know how they have to take the ball out of bounds after a basket? I think they ought to be able to just grab the ball out of the basket and run up court."

Silence from Hearn. The caller had lost all credibility.

Finally, Hearn, with annoyance in his voice, said, "And what's your other idea, buddy?"

"You know how you have eight seconds to get the ball out of your backcourt?"

"Is that a little slow for you?" said Hearn, dropping all pretense of giving serious consideration to the caller. "What would you like, about four seconds? Let me ask you something now. Is your son, Johnny, there?"

"Yes, he is."

"Could I talk to him?"

"Sure!"

There was a rustling of the phone and a high-pitched voice said, tentatively, "H-h-ello."

"Johnny, this is Chick Hearn."

"Oh hi, Mr. Hearn."

"Could you do me a favor?"

"Anything, Mr. Hearn."

"Tell your dad he's an idiot."

DYAN CANNON

Actress

I used to get angry with Chick, I must admit. On the way to Laker games, I would tune in the pregame show. He was so brutally honest that, sometimes, he would put our players down, tell them off, say what they weren't doing right.

When I'd tell him he was making me mad, he would say, "Then don't tune me in."

He wasn't being mean. He just felt people should understand that he was going to talk straight.

BOB SPECK

The first time Bill Walton faced Kareem Abdul-Jabbar, it was in an exhibition game in Cincinnati in 1974. Bill was on the Trail Blazers and Kareem was with the Bucks. I sold the telecast to CBS with the idea that Chick and John Wooden would do the game.

It was perfect because Wooden had coached both Kareem and Bill. The problem was, Wooden had a prior engagement in L.A. So we had him do his part from Los Angeles and Chick from the game, but we didn't tell the audience they were separated. The pregame show was taped in a studio before Chick left.

With Wooden sitting in the L.A. studio, wearing a headset and watching a monitor, and Chick in Cincinnati, you'd swear as a viewer that they were sitting next to each other. We kept the camera on the court and simply avoided showing Chick sitting alone.

There was a tense moment when Wooden's headset went out for 30 seconds. Chick had asked him a question and there was no answer. So

Chick ad-libbed by saying, "Coach Wooden just went out for a glass of water—it's hot as hell in here—but he'll be right back."

No one would have ever known had not Wooden, after finishing the tape-delay broadcast, gone over to the UCLA campus, where he was seen by Pat Healy, son of Jim Healy, who had a nightly sports show in L.A. The telecast was still on the air when Wooden was spotted.

Healy wondered on his next show how John Wooden could be in two places at one time. We never responded.

The only guy who could have pulled that off was Chick Hearn. We knew the broadcast would be good. What difference did it make that Wooden wasn't actually there? If Wooden had not been on the broadcast, it would have lost some of its appeal. The point was to see Walton and Abdul-Jabbar play against each other. What harm was done?

———

Despite all the other things he was doing, Hearn found time, from 1977 to 1992, to fit in the Rebels of the University of Nevada, Las Vegas.

ROSS PORTER
Dodger Broadcaster and Former UNLV Play-by-Play Man

Chick was doing all this pro basketball and you would think he wanted a break, but he loved the game so much, he still wanted to keep his hand in the college game.

Even though he had to come from Laker games, Chick got there early enough to talk to the coaches. You know Chick. He was always at a game earlier than anybody else and he did his homework. The great ones, I have found, find time to do their homework.

DICK MANOOGIAN
Producer of the UNLV Telecasts

Chick did home games for us, first on television and then on a simulcast when radio was added.

We never had negotiations over a contract, never talked about money. At the end of a season, he would say, "Just send me a check for what you think I'm worth."

We would normally play on Thursdays and Saturdays. The Lakers would have a game on Wednesday. Chick would fly to Las Vegas after that game, do ours on Thursday, fly back to L.A. for a Friday Laker game, come back to Las Vegas for our Saturday game, and then go back to L.A. for a Laker game on Sunday, if necessary.

And he would even do it when the Lakers were on the road. One time he went from Cleveland to our game in Las Vegas and then to Atlanta for the Lakers. It was crazy. His energy level was absolutely incredible.

LARRY MERCHANT
National Broadcast Analyst

I was producing a summer pro league show for ESPN many years ago, consisting of six to eight games. I asked Chick, just on a whim, if he would like to do the games. At that time ESPN might have had a million or two million customers. The network was little more than a germinating idea.

Chick did it, and did it for very few dollars. He came with all kinds of charts and names and the backgrounds of the players, preparing as though he was doing the seventh game of the NBA Finals.

JEANIE BUSS

When I was working at the Forum promoting events, one of those events was tennis. They were just starting to air the sport on Prime Ticket, the old cable network. When I heard Chick would be available to do the telecasts, that meant so much to me because it validated that our tennis matches were important events.

He was great on those telecasts. You could tell he had an appreciation for it. Or, if he didn't, you wouldn't know it. He did his homework.

Most people think of him doing football or, of course, basketball, but he could do so many different things.

BOB STEINER
Public Relations Director for California Sports

We were in the press room watching tennis. This was when Chick was doing the sport for Prime Ticket.

"Boy, that Mat-tts Will-ender is really a good tennis player," Chick said.

Correcting the pronunciation, I said Mats Wilander's name phonetically: "M-a-ats V-lander."

Replied Chick, "Whatever."

"And you're our tennis announcer?"

"And," he said, "a damn good one, too."

Which he was.

SCOTT OSTLER
Former Laker Beat Writer for the *Los Angeles Times*

My wife, Kathy, was working with Keith Erickson in a company called Dream Game. The idea was, people would buy audio tapes of simulated Laker games called by Chick in which he would insert their name and a little bit of commentary in a two-minute snippet.

Chick would say something like, "Lakers on the move. Magic dribble drives, passes over in the corner to . . ." and this is where he would insert the name, say, Scott Ostler. "Ostler, the 6'4" forward from Purdue, puts it up. Ostler makes it!"

Chick would go into a studio and do 30 to 40 at a sitting in a couple of hours.

The tapes became popular in Hollywood with some of the stars. One was ordered for comedian John Candy.

One of my wife's jobs was to be in the studio with Chick to make sure he didn't get too far off track, but she wasn't in the booth for the Candy tape.

On there, Chick said, "John Candy's got the ball. The guy's 6'4", but boy, a real fatso, I'll tell you. He's carrying weight, but there he goes, dribbling down the court."

They shipped the tapes out without listening to them. About three weeks later, this guy called the Dream Game office furious. It seems he had been the one to deliver the tape to Candy.

"John Candy's going to fire me," he yelled. "I'm so mad I'm going to sue you guys."

"What's the problem?" he was asked.

"What's the problem? Didn't you listen to that thing? He called John Candy a fatso."

It was just Chick having a little fun, but an apology was quickly forthcoming from the Dream Game office.

———

As he moved from job to job, Hearn never seemed to slow down.

BOB MILLER
L.A. Kings Broadcaster

I always wanted to ask Chick, but I never did, where was he going so fast?

He and I did a 30-second commercial one day. He did the first 15 seconds, I did the second. By the time I was done with my 15 seconds, he was out the door.

"Chick, wait," I yelled, "we've got to check the tape."

I emceed the celebration on the Forum court for Chick's two thousandth consecutive broadcast. Mr. Cooke was there and they had a whole program scripted out.

I introduced Chick at halftime. He walked out to center court, and his first words to me were, "How long is this going to take?"

Where was he going? He still had another half to do.

~ 13 ~
His Travels

The Chick Hearn Show didn't stop merely because the final buzzer sounded in a game or the final one-liner emanated from his microphone. The cast of characters simply expanded. Instead of only Elgin and Magic and Shaq, the straight people in Hearn's never-ending routine also included bus drivers, waitresses, airline pilots, and doormen.

And sportswriters. Always sportswriters.

Even Superman got into the act.

If Gulliver's travels were worthy of a book, Hearn's might be worth several volumes. Willie Nelson would have come up with a new version of "On the Road Again" if he had been part of Ringmaster Chick's Traveling Circus.

Thanks to Hearn, being on road trips was always fun, never dull. Regardless of the Lakers' fortunes at the moment, Hearn managed to keep everybody in the party entertained while leaving behind a trail of bemused objects of his wit. You didn't sign on to be a punch line in the Chick Hearn Show, but once you got the call, there was no avoiding it.

It became increasingly difficult for Hearn to orchestrate that show as the years moved on, not so much because of his age, but rather the circumstances. It was a lot easier to maintain his lighthearted influence over a smaller, unbridled group. When Hearn started, the Lakers and the rest of the traveling party, including the media, were together on commercial flights, stayed in the same hotels, and even, on occasion, all went out to eat as a group.

That had all changed by Hearn's final days. Players were isolated from the media and even from each other if they so chose, flying on charters and often interacting only with the music coming out of the headsets they constantly wore or the cell phones they constantly used.

The following story by Jerry West, of a Hearn moment in the early years, could never happen today.

JERRY WEST
Laker Player, Coach, and Front-Office Executive

I'm sitting on the aisle of our commercial flight, and Chick is sitting across from me with a little old lady next to him.

He starts telling her that he was a flying ace during World War II, that he had shot down some 50 planes and won the Medal of Honor. Then he tells her how he found himself in the middle of four enemy planes shooting at him from four different angles. But somehow, he was able to maneuver his way around them and shoot all four down.

When Chick gets up to go to the bathroom, the lady looks at me and says, "What a brave American."

Chick was such a witty person. Even though he professed to be unbiased, he would get down like the rest of us when things weren't going well with the team. But normally, he kept us in stitches laughing. We really had fun with each other. But those days are gone forever.

Nowadays, we are into the big bad wolf syndrome in regard to the media. We try to separate them from the team as much as possible. Today, the players have bodyguards, posses. The egos are more outrageous.

———

While Hearn may have reveled in keeping a constant laugh track going around him, he was deadly serious when it came to basketball. Nothing was more important than the Lakers.

I learned that lesson on one of my first road trips with the team. It was to Seattle in the spring of 1980 for a pair of playoff games.

On game day, the players head to the arena for a morning shootaround, religiously attended by Hearn. I figured I would see enough of the Lakers that night.

What I preferred to see were the remains of the old city of Seattle, the crumbling ruins beneath the surface of the modern city, reachable on a daily tour.

It also sounded like a good idea to Scott Ostler, a fellow writer, so we booked a morning tour, only to have the story of our expedition to the dead city passed on to Hearn.

When someone yelled out to us in the hotel lobby as we were leaving, Hearn broke in.

"Oh, leave them alone," he said with mock disgust. "They are tourists."

For a man who liked to get to the arena four hours before the opening tip-off, there was no time for tours.

HOWARD BECK
Laker Beat Writer for the *Los Angeles Daily News*

It was my second year on the beat. I knew what Chick was about in terms of his streak, about coming to work every day, about always being there no matter what else was happening. But I didn't realize how much he projected that on everybody else around him.

Right after the lockout in 1998, the Lakers and the Clippers were scheduled to play two exhibition games back to back at the Arrowhead Pond in Anaheim. I skipped the first night because it was my girlfriend's birthday. I went the second night, walked into the press room, grabbed something to eat, sat down, and Chick walked in.

"Where were you last night?" he asked.

"What?" I replied.

"Where were you?"

"What do you mean?"

"You weren't at the game last night."

"Chick, it was my girlfriend's birthday, and it's a long season."

"Awww, that's no excuse," he said. "You should have been here."

It was an *exhibition* game, an exhibition game against the *Clippers* in Anaheim. Nothing could have been more meaningless, less important.

Except to Chick. It wasn't an exhibition game to him. It was a game. Period. And if it's our job to be there, we must be there.

Chick needled those who didn't share his unwavering devotion to all things Laker, although he was still supportive of their career goals.

When I first started traveling with the Lakers, Chick singled me out as the straight man for many of his zingers, as he had done with other rookie writers. It was sort of like being targeted by Don Rickles. You felt special.

Buses often became the stage for Hearn's shtick, and I often played a role.

Like the night in Boston when I put my wallet down on my hotel nightstand. Before dropping off to sleep, I made a call and then put the phone down on that nightstand, right on top of my wallet.

We had one of those 7:00 A.M. departures the next morning, the kind where you pack with one eye still shut. In my sleep-deprived condition, I didn't realize I had left my wallet behind until our bus was cruising toward the airport.

A panicked call was made, and a hotel employee returned the wallet before our flight was airborne.

No harm, no foul?

Don't be silly. We're talking about Chick Hearn.

He didn't say anything about the embarrassing incident for a while—not on the flight, not on our arrival in the next city, not until we were on another bus heading to yet another hotel.

"Hey, Riles," Hearn finally yelled to Pat Riley, then the Laker coach, who was seated a few rows ahead. "Next time we go to Boston, I got a great new hotel we ought to stay at."

"Really? Which one?" asked Riley.

"Oh, never mind," Hearn said. "I forgot. They have wall phones there. Springer would have no place to leave his wallet."

One afternoon, on a team bus in Denver, I was sitting behind Hearn, carrying on a loud conversation that was obviously annoying him.

How do I know that? Because he let me know when we pulled up at an intersection where a workman was applying a jackhammer to the asphalt.

"Hey, Springer," Hearn said loudly enough to be assured everyone was listening, "do you want to make some extra money?"

I answered on cue as any straight man would, "Yes, Chick."

"Well then," he said, "get out there, put your chin on the sidewalk, and start talking."

LYNN SHACKELFORD
Former Laker Broadcast Analyst

Wilt Chamberlain's salary was revealed in the paper one day. Chick saw it while we were on the bus, but didn't say anything until he saw Jerry West had read that item and grown quiet.

Then, Chick told Jerry, "I didn't know Wilt was making that much. Did you?"

Replied Jerry, "The owner and I are going to have to have a talk when we get back."

Chick looked at Connie Hawkins and said, "Connie, when you are through looking at the pictures, can I have the paper?"

FRANK O'NEILL
Former Laker Trainer

One of Chick's favorite things was to get the bus drivers caught up in his gags.

One day in Phoenix, we passed a sign advertising dog food. He and Wilt Chamberlain started arguing about which brand of dog food was better.

"I've tasted them all and this is the best," Wilt said.

"You're crazy," said Chick, making sure the driver could hear them talk.

"No, believe me, I've tasted them all."

That poor driver got so wrapped up in the conversation, he missed the turnoff.

BILL SHARMAN
Laker Coach and Front-Office Executive

Wilt Chamberlain and Chick were always the first two on the bus back to the hotel after a game. Wilt would sit in the front row, Chick in the second row. And they would decide who, other than players, would get on the bus, whether it was writers or family or friends of the other Lakers.

So Wilt became known as the sheriff and Chick as his deputy.

One night, sportswriter Larry Stewart tried to board the bus, only to find Wilt's long legs blocking him.

"Who are you, my man?" asked Wilt in that booming voice of his.

Stewart told him.

"Chick," said Wilt, "is he OK?"

Chick took a dramatic pause and then said, "Yeah, I guess we should let him on."

JOSH ROSENFELD
Former Laker Public Relations Director

Chick was one of the greatest tormentors of bus drivers of all time.

———

But he was an equal-opportunity tormentor. Nobody escaped his good-natured barbs.

There was the morning in Indianapolis when I found Hearn in the hotel coffee shop enthusiastically devouring an omelette.

"That looks good," I said as I sat down. "I think I'll get one."

A waitress came over to take my order, but I never got a chance to give it.

"He'll have what I had," Hearn told the waitress, "but he'd like his eggs warm."

The waitress, not noticing the twinkle in Hearn's eyes, was horrified.

"Oh, Mr. Hearn," she said, "I'm sorry. Is there something else I can get you?"

"No, you already ruined my day," he said. "See what you can do for him."

The waitress wouldn't be denied.

"There must be something I can get you," she said.

"All right," he said, "bring me a stomach pump."

At that point, his timing impeccable as always, Hearn abandoned the gag and broke into a big smile, letting the waitress in on the fun.

Taxi drivers, too, could unknowingly become part of the Chick Show.

JOHNNY WEST
Jerry West's Son

In Philadelphia for the NBA Finals in 2001, we were returning from dinner one night in a cab, Chick, Marge, Shannon, my mom [Karen], and I. As we pulled up, the driver of our cab said, "You know, the Lakers are staying at your hotel."

"Oh really?" Chick said. "Who are they?"

"A professional basketball team," the driver said.

Then the driver told us, "I saw Mitch Kupchak the other day."

Chick said, "And who's he?"

Chick really had the driver going the whole time. He had no idea who Chick was.

MICHAEL VENTRE
MSNBC Sports Columnist

I started covering the Lakers in the fall of 1983. In those days, they trained in Palm Desert and stayed at Jerry Buss' Ocotillo Lodge in Palm Springs.

Having arrived in town late in the evening, I made plans to have a drink at the hotel with Josh Rosenfeld, then the Lakers' media relations director and an old friend.

It was 11:30 at night, and I kind of remembered where Josh's room was, but I wasn't positive. I went to what I thought was his room and started knocking and knocking and knocking.

Finally, the door opened and it was Chick, bleary-eyed and in his pajamas. He started mumbling, "Who? Huh? What?"

I responded awkwardly, "Oh, Chick, I'm so sorry to wake you up. I was looking for Josh's room."

"Don't worry about it," Chick said. "I'll take care of it."

By then I realized my mistake. Josh was in the next room over. But Chick was so insistent and so helpful and so great. He said, "Come on, I'll find out where it is," and proceeded to call the front desk.

I was standing there so embarrassed. This was the first time I was meeting this legend, and I woke him up out of a sound sleep.

The next day, I walked into the gym at Palm Desert where the Lakers trained, and there was Chick, sitting with Jerry West. I was terrified because I thought Chick was really going to give it to me. Instead, Chick called me over, patted me on the back, and said, "How are you? Good to see you. Welcome to the beat. Do you have any questions? Let me show you around."

He couldn't have been nicer.

The following day, I again walked into practice, and Chick was again sitting in the same spot across the gym.

This time, he yelled out, for everybody to hear, "Thanks for letting me get a night's sleep, Ventre."

He had given me a one-day grace period.

STEVE BISHEFF
Orange County Register Sports Columnist

I was a rookie on the beat, the Lakers were in Boston, and I ended up driving to the game with Chick and Mal Florence, a *Los Angeles Times* sportswriter. A relative kid in the business, I had never been to Boston Garden. I had no idea where we were going. All I know is that I expected Boston Garden to be Boston Garden.

We walked into a building, and there's a train station there.

Chick looked at me and said, "So, you ready to get on a train?"

"A train?" I said. "What are you talking about?"

He and Mal carried this on for four or five minutes until they both finally broke up with laughter.

"You're just a kid," said Chick between laughs. "Such a raw rookie. Don't worry. We take an elevator and go upstairs to the Garden. It's above the station."

He asked me to be on the pregame show that day. I wanted to make a good impression, so I told all my friends back home to watch, and then Chick said on the air, "The kid didn't even know where the Boston Garden was."

He loved doing that, but he was kind. It was never mean-spirited. When he did that to you, it almost made you feel as if you belonged.

ELGIN BAYLOR
Former Laker

When it came to kidding, Chick was the best. He was always trying to pull a fast one. He'd come up to you in the airport and tell you our flight had been canceled because of the weather. He'd be real serious. He'd see you coming down into the lobby with your bags and he'd tell you the game had been called off. He'd come up with just anything. You'd never know.

He had fun doing it, but he'd never do anything malicious.

MITCH CHORTKOFF
Former Laker Beat Writer for the *Santa Monica Outlook*

At the end of a long trip, I look in my wallet as we are landing and I see that I only have five dollars. Considering how long my car has been parked at the airport, it's going to cost a lot more than that. I say to Chick, "I hate to ask you, but I don't think I can bail out my car. Can I borrow $20?"

"Oh, no problem. Anytime."

He gives me $20, but, of course, with Chick, there's always a string attached.

The next night, the Lakers are playing at the Forum and I'm in my usual courtside press seat. During the game, the ball comes bouncing up on the press table and knocks the phone in front of me off its hook. I reach over and put it back on.

Broadcasting from above, Chick tells his audience, "Well, there was a call for Mitch Chortkoff, which is a good thing, because he didn't have a dime to make his own call."

———

There was one night when not even Hearn could come up with a snappy one-liner. But then, it was no laughing matter.

LYNN SHACKELFORD

Because of a bad snowstorm, our flight is diverted from Cleveland to Toledo. We're hungry when we get in, so Chick and Frank O'Neill and I go to an all-night diner.

The only empty seats are at the counter. There are two open, then a guy sitting in the next seat over, then another empty one. I ask the guy sitting alone to move down one so all three of us can sit together.

As we're eating, Chick looks up and says, "Hey, a police car just pulled up."

We don't pay much attention. Then another comes screeching up. And another. The police come racing in, guns drawn, and order everybody over to the wall.

Except Chick. They point their guns at him and tell him to put his hands in the air.

"I think he's serious," Chick says.

We don't know what's going on until finally the waitress comes over and says, "No, not him. The other guy," pointing to the man who had given us his seat.

It turned out the guy had come in and demanded apple pie and ice cream, telling the waitress he had a gun. She had snuck off, called the police, and told them the guy was sitting in the third seat from the entrance.

Which is where Chick sat down after the guy had politely moved.

A normal Hearn meal was better planned. And eaten in a far better environment. Diners weren't normally his thing.

Susan Stratton
Hearn's Producer and Director for a Quarter of a Century

We would always go to lunch on game day on the road and talk about the show. Chick was a treat to eat with. He liked nice restaurants. They had to have white tablecloths. He would pick the best table and reserve it.

When you went with Chick, you were his honored guest. You didn't do a thing. You just kind of walked along and there you were. We would get to the door and the maitre d' would come over and take us over to this reserved table. God forbid the table was not ready, or someone else had it because that was going to be World War III.

Chick didn't like bad food. If it was bad, he would let them know it.

He used to love to go down to breakfast early in the morning. He'd be the first person in the restaurant, or might even be waiting for them to open the door. And if they didn't open promptly, he'd let them know that, too.

Bill Bertka
Laker Assistant Coach

He was the first one on the plane, he was the first one off the plane. He was the first one in the hotel, the first one in his room. The next day, you reverse it. If you're going back to the airport, he was the first one on the bus.

Stu Lantz
Laker Broadcast Analyst

I said to him, "Do you ever sleep?" We'd get into places late at night and he'd be the first one down to breakfast. You just never saw him sleep.

If he would say, "Let's go to the arena at 4:30," I'm telling you, at 4:10, 4:15, he's in the lobby, sitting in a chair, waiting on me. I'd come down at 4:25 and he'd say, "Oh, you finally showed up, huh?"

"It's 4:25," I'd tell him. "You said 4:30."

"Well, I've been down here since 10 minutes after 4:00."

"Then why didn't you tell me you wanted to leave at 4:15?"

BILL BERTKA

You could set your watch by Chick's routines. I would usually be one of the last ones to go up the elevator to my room when we checked in.

But I always knew one thing. As I went up to my room, Chick would be coming down to go to the front desk, mumbling, "They gave me a room right next to the ice machine," or, "They gave me a room right next to the elevator. I can't even hear the TV."

One time, I said to him, "Chick, what's wrong?"

He said, "My room is too small. I walked in and almost fell out the window."

MITCH KUPCHAK
Laker Player and General Manager

Remember, at one time Chick was actually the assistant general manager. Right to the end, if he didn't get the room he liked, he would switch from an announcer to an assistant general manager at the front desk.

One time, he was complaining to the front-desk clerk that his room was next to the elevator, or didn't overlook the park, or whatever was wrong with it. "Don't you know who I am?" he said. "I'm the assistant general manager of this club."

"Well, it says *announcer* next to your name," he was told.

"No, I'm the assistant general manager, and you have to learn to take care of the right people."

———

When the Cavaliers played in Richfield, Ohio, outside Cleveland, the Lakers stayed in a wooded area near the arena in a hotel that was only one step up from a minimum-security prison.

There was nothing within walking distance except a Dairy Queen, and the weather was usually so harsh when the Lakers were there that the finest gourmet restaurant wouldn't have been worth that walk.

On one trip, the Lakers arrived on a Monday around noon, more than 30 hours before their Tuesday night game. Nearly everybody in the traveling party gathered at the hot dog stand in the hotel, purchased lunch, and sat in a semicircle eating.

When lunch was finished, it was 12:30.

Now what?

Rich Levin, the beat writer from the *Herald-Examiner,* stood up and announced, "I'm going to my room to kill myself."

There were a few chuckles and then a couple of minutes of silence.

Finally, Hearn stood up and said, "Which way is Rich's room?"

MARY LOU LIEBICH
Laker Administrative Assistant

The choice of our hotels was not his. Chick could complain about it, but it didn't do him any good. But he did complain.

A lot.

One time, the Lakers, on a trip to New York, had just arrived at a hotel the team had not used before. Chick could not possibly have been in his room for more than a few minutes when he called me.

"Mary," he said, "what are you doing? What kind of a hotel did you put us in?"

"What do you mean?" I said.

"I'm staring out my window and I'm looking at a billboard advertising some kind of weird sex."

———

One night in Philadelphia, Hearn got into an elevator with several reporters. The door opened at the second floor and a man in a Superman costume entered. The elevator stopped again at the third floor and Superman got out.

As the door closed, Chick said, "You'd think the silly son of a gun could have jumped that high."

STU LANTZ

Chick had this thin cardboard he would use to make up a spotting chart for each team, each and every game. He carried it with him along with different colored pens and a pair of scissors.

He's working late one night in some city, doesn't matter which one, making up this chart. He gets tired, so he just lays the stuff on the nightstand and goes to sleep.

He hadn't checked the alarm on the clock radio, however. As it turned out, whoever had used the room before him had left the alarm set.

Well, that alarm starts ringing at 4:00 in the morning. It's still dark. Chick's trying to reach for the off button, but he can't get to it. So he grabs his scissors and cuts the cord to the clock. Instead of pulling the plug out of the wall, he just cuts the cord.

When he told me that story, I said, "Do you know how dangerous that could be? You are cutting through wiring."

MARY LOU LIEBICH

After a loss on the road, Chick would call the next day and say, "What did you think of that one?"

"It was pretty bad, Chick," I would tell him.

"It was worse than that," he would say.

Several decades ago, airport security was largely nonexistent. But that didn't mean an airport couldn't be a hazardous place for a clueless writer traveling with Hearn.

SCOTT OSTLER
Former Laker Beat Writer for the *Los Angeles Times*

There were four of us in a rental car heading to the airport in the midst of a road trip, Chick and three writers: myself, Rich Levin of the *Herald-Examiner*, and Mitch Chortkoff of the *Santa Monica Outlook*.

Next stop: Houston. As we drove up to the terminal, Chick gave each of us our assignment. One of us was supposed to turn in the car, another get the tickets, and so on.

My assignment was to check in the luggage. Dropped off at curbside, I took the bags, gave them to the guy with the red cap, and said, "These go to Houston."

When we got to Houston, the four of us went to the baggage carousel to await our luggage. We were standing there talking, joking, laughing. But as the minutes passed and everybody else started disappearing with their bags, our frivolity cooled down because none of our bags were showing up. Pretty soon, we were the only four people left.

Chick was staring at me as if I were a criminal. I had messed up somehow. I shrugged and said, "What?"

"Let me see those baggage tags," Chick barked.

I handed them to him and he quickly ascertained that the luggage had been sent to the wrong airline. I had said "Houston," but somehow, the baggage guy had thought I said, "Eastern." So he put them on an Eastern Airlines flight, and we were flying United or American. I don't remember which one.

I do remember that sinking feeling I was experiencing. There was a game that night, and Chick had all his suits and makeup and everything in those bags. It wasn't as if he was going to have to go on TV in a wifebeater's T-shirt or anything, but you know Chick. He was extremely mad.

We had plenty of time to dash over to the Eastern baggage area and claim our stuff, so it was not a total tragedy.

As we were walking over there, Chick looked at me and snarled to Rich, "Put a leash on that bleepety bleep and let's get out of here."

———

Being anxious at an airport was normal for Hearn.

FRANK O'NEILL

He always wanted to leave as early as possible. If we had an 8:00 flight, he'd say, "Why not the 7:00?" He always wanted to change. Fred [Schaus] finally gave him his own airline schedule as a gift.

LYNN SHACKELFORD

As soon as there would be the slightest mechanical problem, Chick would say, "These airline people are not being truthful with us. We'd better get off and find another flight." Or, if we were on a connecting flight, he'd say, "Isn't there a nonstop?"

One time in Buffalo, it appeared we were not going to be able to get out on our commercial flight. So I checked into charters. The best I could do, as I told Chick, was to get several planes that could hold four passengers each.

"We want a plane," he said, "not a fleet."

FRANK O'NEILL

Shackelford used to keep everything related to travel neatly arranged in a briefcase. One of Chick's favorite pranks was to pick that briefcase up and shake it violently, mixing everything up. Shackelford would go crazy.

GARY VITTI
Laker Trainer
When I first came to the team, I was told I would be the traveling secretary, but I didn't know how to do all that stuff. Chick taught me everything.

In those days, we flew on commercial airliners, so we had to take the first flight out. It didn't make any difference what time I got down to the lobby in the morning. If I got there at 5:30 A.M., Chick was there at 5:15. If I got there at 5:15, he was there at 5:00, sitting with his newspaper and his cup of coffee. We had to get going that early because the flights would be around 7:00.

He'd take a cab with me to the airport, both of us freezing our butts off. Once we got there, he'd help me separate the boarding passes for everybody. He'd talk to the skycaps. He knew everybody in the airport and everybody knew him. The guy was unbelievable.

SUSAN STRATTON

Chick was going with the team to Las Vegas for a preseason game. But when he got to the airport, there was a problem with the plane.

He got so disgusted, he walked over to the ticket counter of another airline, got on a plane, and left.

Stu [Lantz] stayed with the team, flew to Las Vegas, and, when he got off the elevator on his floor in the Luxor Hotel, there was Chick in the hallway, trying to find his room. After all that, they had gotten there at the same time.

Hearn was seated next to a woman who had a camera in her lap on a commercial flight. I was seated across the aisle, engrossed in a conversation.

"Hey, lady," said Hearn, "want to make a quick 20 bucks?"

The woman, looking shocked, replied, "What do I have to do?"

Pointing in my direction, Hearn said, "Get me a picture of him with his mouth closed."

RICK FOX
Laker Forward

He would come and sit behind me in the card games on the plane. He could have sat behind anybody, but he sat behind me. He would watch my cards and comment. It was basically play-by-play of a card game.

And my luck would always seem to change when he showed up. So that would make some of the guys who started losing say, "Go sit down, Chick."

DEL HARRIS
Former Laker Coach

Whenever things were dragging on the plane as far as taking off, he and I had a little thing going. I'd say, "Chick, what do you think? Are you ready to go?" And Chick would yell out real loud, "Le-e-et's, g-o-o-o-o!"

We probably did that routine 50, 60 times.

RICK FOX

Chick had a love for a schedule. Once he yelled "Let's go," it was time to go.

DEREK FISHER
Laker Guard

It got to the point where, if Chick didn't say "Let's go," we knew something was wrong.

Now that he's gone, when we're on a plane, Rudy [Garciduenas], our equipment manager, or somebody else will yell it out just for old time's sake.

LINDA RAMBIS
Kurt Rambis' Wife and a Member of the Laker Front-Office Staff

The travel takes a toll on you. Kurt comes home and he's exhausted from the road. You're taking flights and you're not sleeping in your own bed. Now they travel on charter flights, but there were 30 plus years when they were on commercial flights, sometimes squashed in coach. They would take the very first flight out in the morning, traveling in winter, carrying their luggage, doing all that schlepping around.

It also takes an emotional toll. You're missing all the milestones in your family. But Chick lived and breathed it.

I can't imagine my husband, who is a physically fit ex-athlete, doing this for that many years. It takes a remarkable person with incredible stamina to do that job for over 40 years.

Stu Lantz

I couldn't believe what he did. I was amazed at how he could respond to all of the travel, all the late hours, sleeping in strange beds, the different eating habits you develop on the road.

It never affected him in how he did his job. I would think that, at his age, you would be able to sense it in some way, but I never could. He was a marvel to me, truly a marvel.

He might bitch by saying, "Oh, we're going to get in at 3:00 in the morning," but once the next day came and it was time for a game, he would act like it was the first game of his career. He was always gung-ho about doing the games.

———

Chick's magical tour is over. The new generation of Lakers and sportswriters and bus drivers and all the rest are on their own.

~ 14 ~
His Fans

Celebrities or nobodies, the guy in the courtside seat or the guy in the nose-bleed section, the kid with the radio pressed to his ear in bed or the senior with the television blaring in his rest home—Chick Hearn had a way of touching them all.

What follows is a cross section of those who will forever hear the voice of the Lakers in their head, thus preserving a priceless era.

DYAN CANNON
Actress

I would bring him brownies about every third game. He commentated on a celebrity game I played in. I wanted him to comment on my free throws, but all he would comment on was my legs.

He helped me understand the game better. I was just so blessed to know this incredible man. And I sit next to Magic courtside, so I had two professors all the time to teach me the subtleties of the game.

ROBERT GOULET
Entertainer

In a 1966 telegram to Hearn:

> Dear Chick, Thank you for making the games even more exciting and interesting than they are.

Chick

PENNY MARSHALL
Actress and Director
Look in the Laker program. They have Stu Lantz and Paul Sunderland mixed up. Each of their names is under the other one's picture. They wouldn't do that with Chick.

KEITH ERICKSON
Former Laker Broadcast Analyst
Fans would come up to him in every city to say how much they enjoyed the broadcasts, how he made every game so great. That happened every single place we went.

I don't think Chick had any idea how much people loved him.

SHERON BELLIO
Producer, Laker Talk Show
He'd be on the air and a little kid would come up to get his autograph. The security guard would shoo the kid away.

I didn't realize it, but Chick would be watching the whole thing while he was on the air. When he'd get off, he'd get an usher to go get the kid. He knew where the kid was because he'd watch him walk back to his seat. Chick would take off his championship ring and let the kid hold it.

There were always people coming up, wanting autographs, wanting to take pictures, and he never turned anybody away. The fans were so important to him.

MARY LOU LIEBICH
Laker Administrative Assistant
He was really good about autographs. And not everyone in his position is. Some get really bothered or are on an ego trip.

If there was someone in a wheelchair, Chick would be happy to meet with them before the game.

LON ROSEN
Sports Agent
People from all over the country would recognize Chick and he would always be receptive.

They would ask him to reminisce about games in the sixties, seventies, eighties, nineties, or right up to that game. And Chick always gave people whatever time they needed.

They had a Chick bobblehead night a few years ago. I was there with my young sons, Brian and Michael. Chick saw us sitting in our seats without bobbleheads, so he sent somebody over with two of them.

STEVE CHASE
Laker Fantasy Camp Operator
It made no difference whether he was talking to the president of IBM or the cleanup crew at Staples Center. Chick treated everybody the same, treated everybody like they were the president of the United States.

STU LANTZ
Laker Broadcast Analyst
After a preseason game in Honolulu, Chick and I were on our merry way out of the arena parking lot in our rental car, with Chick driving, when we found the street blocked.

You could normally go both ways, but after a game, it was one way only. Our hotel was to the left, but you could only go right. Now you could turn right, go around the block, and be headed in the proper direction.

Not Chick.

With all the other cars going right, Chick put his left blinker on and started edging in that direction.

And do you know, those people recognized him, stopped, and let him pull down the side of the street to the left until we could get clear.

Marge Hearn

His idea of a good time on a free day at home was for us to go out, have dinner and a few drinks, and talk to the bartenders. We rarely discussed the Lakers with them. He just loved bartenders.

James Worthy
Former Laker

He would call up one of his favorite bartenders at halftime of a game and ask him how he had sounded in the first half. He was just a people person.

Randy Levitz
Fan

I used to come by Chick's broadcast area in the days I was in law school and say hello.

I told him I was going to try to pass the bar exam, and the next time I saw him, he asked me how I had done. I told him I had failed.

"Don't worry," he said with a smile, "I never pass a bar, either."

———

Marge Hearn received thousands of letters upon the death of her husband. A few samples follow.

Jo Skibby
Newport Beach Children's Learning Center

Chick Hearn was not only the voice of the L.A. Lakers, but a voice for all kinds of people.

Those around Chick's broadcast spot knew when to assist him to the aisle, where he would respond to a parent's request to encourage a son or daughter's school work or even to look at a report card. I've heard Chick say to a student, "Now bring me the next report card, because I know you are going to improve even more."

On other occasions, I observed Chick interact with persons who had physical issues: quadruple amputee, cerebral palsy, or mental retardation, among others. His genuine words of care for these people warmed my heart and brought tears to my eyes as he spoke to them with compassion.

DENNIS CYPHER

When I was a high school basketball player, I would put Chick on the radio when I was practicing outside and pretend that I was playing in the game he was calling. My then girlfriend, and now wife of 37 years, would call me "the littlest Laker."

She loves to tell the story of the first night of our honeymoon. Chick went with us, as I had to have the Laker game on in our hotel room.

GARY JAMES

In 1956, when I was 10 years old, I was hit by a car while waiting to cross the street to search for lost baseballs in Peoria, Illinois.

Chick discussed my hit-and-run accident on his sports show. Because of that, I got a great big hat box full of cards and gifts.

I have told the story fondly of the man who took the time to say something about a young boy with a passion for baseball. It has meant more to me as each year passes.

CHRIS ZEARING

When I was five years old, my dad, a scoutmaster for the Boy Scouts, would take me on Boy Scout camping trips. I remember we would listen to Chick announce the games on a little, battery-operated television in our tent.

It was a special time for my dad and me.

JEFFREY MOUALIM

Chick was my saving grace many times. Because I have hemophilia, I spent many, many days and nights at home, and what helped get me through those tough times was looking forward to Chick's broadcast of Laker games.

Chick was gracious enough to grant me an interview for my high school newspaper in 1971. For a 15-year-old boy, it was a life-changing experience.

TRICIA MALONEY

Marge, I had the pleasure of meeting you and Chick at my store in Encino four years ago. I will always remember Chick taking off his championship ring and allowing me to try it on. I have told that story to everyone I know, and their response is always, "It sounds like Chick."

DON LECHMAN

There was nothing like turning on Chick on a dull, cold January night and listening to his warm, friendly tones bringing every detail of a Laker game to life. He was like my best friend for every night from October through June.

What will I do now that he is gone? What will you do, Marge? Well, you will do just fine. You're tough. The rest of us, I don't know. . . . The Lakers could win every game, Jerry West could come back in uniform, Magic could be miraculously cured and 21 again, and none of that would be the same as Chick coming back.

Chick made every game exciting and enjoyable, no matter the score. When he was bored, he would let us know it, but somehow, he never bored us.

CATHY WHITTAKER

I used to always say, if I ever go blind, just play Chick Hearn tapes for me, and I'll think I can still see.

HAROLD GUYE

Marge, in the late fifties or early sixties, my wife and I had the pleasure of seeing you and Chick at a motel in Paso Robles. You were walking together with your arms around each other's waists. Joyce, my wife, turned to me and said, "Look at that couple. They are so obviously in love. Isn't that a delight to see?"

Please take solace in the fact that you had a marriage that lasted longer than most people's lives.

Mark Walch

I remember Chick used to dedicate games "to all you shut-ins out there." I took this for granted until I myself became a shut-in for several months in the early eighties.

Then, I felt as if Chick were talking to me.

Josh Rosenfeld
Former Laker Public Relations Director

I'm sitting in a restaurant on the road with Chick and some writers when this fan comes up to tell Chick how much his 80-year-old mother loves listening to him from her retirement home, and could Chick somehow say hello to her on the air?

Sure, Chick tells him, just write her name down and he'd be happy to do it.

The excited fan writes the name on a slip of paper, says good-bye, and leaves.

When he is barely out of sight, Chick tears the paper into many pieces and flings them in the air, drawing much laughter from the writers.

As we walk out, I glance back and there is Chick, on all fours under the table, picking up those torn scraps and putting them back together.

He had enjoyed putting on a show for his media friends, but he certainly didn't intend to let that fan and the 80-year-old mother suffer for it.

———

Even among the often cynical media, Hearn's fans were legion.

J. A. ADANDE
Los Angeles Times Columnist

I started off on the road to becoming the next Chick Hearn and I got side-tracked a little bit. I wanted to be that guy sitting in his seat. Until a few years ago, I used to think, "If I had stayed on that path, I'd still be waiting."

Bob Miller said he and Chick used to sit back and marvel about how many generations of aspiring broadcasters have come and gone, hoping to wait out Chick and Bob.

The first time I went to the Forum to see the Lakers was in the 1981–1982 season. A sixth grader, I came early with my mother, Elizabeth. We were practically the only people in the building. Chick was up there, practicing for the game. I went up there, got to meet him and stand next to him, and he signed my program. I was a huge Magic fan. Right before the game, they announced Magic had had a death in the family and he wasn't going to be there. But at least I got to meet Chick. That turned out to be the highlight of the day.

One of the privileges of working at the *L.A. Times* was being in the same press room—I won't say the same level—with Chick.

After all those nights at home and those car rides listening to him, now he was actually reading what I had to say. And apparently enjoying it. I probably got more compliments from Chick Hearn than from anyone else in the business. And for me to get compliments from the guy who inspired me to go into sports journalism was just incredible. That was the best reward I could have asked for.

One day, he just came up to me and said, "You are great." Those three words—think of the millions of words Chick Hearn said—meant the world to me.

BRIAN GOLDEN
Antelope Valley Press Columnist

In December of 1984 I went down to Houston because I thought Kareem Abdul-Jabbar's first game against Houston's twin towers [Hakeem Olajuwon and Ralph Sampson] was a big story.

With a sudden snowstorm dropping 18 inches in the Antelope Valley—one of those desert storms—I got out just before the roads closed.

I walked into the press room in Houston and there was Chick. He kind of knew my face because I'd covered some games.

I mentioned the storm to Mr. Hearn—he was trying to coach me to call him Chick, but I felt like I was in the presence of royalty—telling him it was snowing like mad.

The guys back in my office were watching the game, and, right in the middle of the broadcast, Chick said, "And my good friend, Brian Golden, tells me it's snowing pretty heavily in the Antelope Valley, so be careful everybody. Just pull up a chair and watch Laker basketball."

Everybody at our paper was in awe that Chick Hearn had mentioned my name. When I got back, everybody asked me, "Do you know Chick Hearn? He said you were his good friend."

JOHN NADEL
Associated Press

What I remember most about Chick was not what he did during the games. It was after the games at the old Forum. He'd be behind the bar in the press lounge, fixing drinks, rollicking around, talking to everybody, running the show. He was the maestro, just like Magic was the maestro on the court.

I also remember the seventies, when I was working at a newspaper up in Santa Barbara. I presented awards at an annual banquet in June for the best athletes in the Santa Barbara area. I would be the straight man and Chick would be the guest speaker, knock the crowd on its socks, and then talk afterward for half an hour or 45 minutes. He just loved it.

BRIAN GOLDEN

I was asked to do a piece for a newsletter that goes out to Laker season-ticket holders. In it, I wrote:

> The Lakers have had the George Mikan era, the Sports
> Arena era with Doris Day, the Wilt Chamberlain era, the

Kareem era, and now they've got the Shaquille era. But those are all mere subplots of the ultimate story of Laker basketball, which is the Chick Hearn era.

When it came out, Chick called me at home and said, "Brian, I just saw this story and I just wanted to tell you, this is one of the nicest stories that was ever written about me."

I almost dropped the phone.

"Well, Chick, it's true," I told him. "The greatest Dodger of them all is Vin Scully, and the greatest Laker of them all is you."

There was this pause. Did he hang up? Did he not hear me?

Finally, he said, "That's so flattering."

BOB BAKER
Los Angeles Times Reporter

I have this wonderful moment frozen in time from 1962 when Jerry West steals an in-bounds pass in the NBA Finals against the Celtics with three seconds left and goes in for the layup that wins the game. It would be one thing if I'd watched the replay over and over, as we do now. But there was no replay back then. And the game wasn't on TV. I never saw it. But I heard Chick describe it. And the sheer density of detail and intensity he employed went straight to a special place in my head, or maybe it was my heart.

If you're lucky as a kid, you get exposed to a teacher or a mentor who is filled with a sense of urgency, someone who makes you understand that what you do, or what happens around you, or what you think about it, matters tremendously.

That's what Chick did. I would fall asleep listening to the games, games in which every possession was crucial, possessions in which anything might happen, so you had to be on guard. The players would commit impossibly grand acts and, much to Chick's horror, impossibly boneheaded plays. Not only that, but at least a half-dozen times a game, one of those grand acts or miscues would be something Chick seemed to have never seen before. He had, of course, seen such plays many times before, but by responding with fresh enthusiasm, he made me feel that way, too.

Radio is—well, radio is just so cool. In the hands of a master, it sucks you in. It mattered to me that Chick thought Hetzel and Wetzel on the court at the same time for the Lakers created a pronunciation problem for him. It mattered that once Lucius Allen hurt himself slipping on a stray jersey dropped too close to the sideline, Chick would never fail to notice a stray jersey again without reminding us of what happened to Lucius. It mattered that nobody could ever shoot the ball a little too hard, where it bounced straight up off the heel of the rim, without Chick remembering the Don Nelson bounce—remembering it ruefully, the way other people remember the Kennedy assassination when they drive by the Texas book depository.

I learned to be obsessed from Chick. I learned to trust my instincts and become a zealot, whether it made me look geeky or not. I learned that, while there are certainly times to be cool, there are many, many more times where it's better not to be cool, where it's better to care, cajole, argue, celebrate, cry. I learned how to watch basketball in my sleep from listening to Chick, and I learned how to measure life from him, too.

~ 15 ~

His Passing

At the end, it was again just the two of them, driving down a California highway through a lonely stretch of desert, with nearly three-quarters of a century of memories behind them. And the end of the road ahead.

"I think you can be a big help to Kayla someday," said Chick, referring to his great-granddaughter.

What a strange way to put it, thought Marge, leaving himself out like that.

Then Chick said something that really caused her head to turn.

"I think maybe I'd like to spend more time at home with you," he told her.

"Good, then make this season coming up your last," Marge replied.

"I think I will," Chick said.

In the season just completed, Hearn had been forced to end his cherished broadcast streak at 3,338 straight games, had undergone both heart and hip surgery, and had amazed doctors by returning to announce the Lakers' victory in the NBA Finals, which gave them a three-peat. And as if that weren't enough, Hearn had driven to Las Vegas to take his usual spot in a fantasy camp at season's end.

Now, when this leisure drive was over, it would finally be time to kick back into one of his favorite activities: relaxing by the pool of his Encino home.

He had been through prostate cancer, serious knee problems, and all those bouts with laryngitis, but in the waning days of 2001, at the start of his 42nd season behind the Laker microphone, Hearn's heart, which had kept him going through it all, began to let him down.

193

SUSAN STRATTON
Hearn's Producer and Director for a Quarter of a Century

About two weeks before Chick had the operation on his heart, Al McCoy, the Phoenix announcer, had a special luncheon prior to a Laker-Sun game, and he asked Chick to make an appearance.

Chick never did anything on game day, but he agreed to that because it was Al.

Chick was so sick, he couldn't walk.

It had gotten to the point where we had the producer who travels with us, Russell Kodani, meet Chick with a cart at the media room and drive him as close to the floor as he could. Chick still had to walk to his table.

People have no idea just how difficult it was for him in the later years, what he did.

That afternoon in Phoenix, he had so much trouble walking, but he made that luncheon for Al.

MARGE HEARN

At the house one day in December, Fran told me his chest felt heavy. We went to see our doctor, Jack Patterson, who told Fran he had had a very slight heart attack.

Hearn was also told he had a blocked aortic valve and couldn't afford to wait until the end of the season, perhaps six months away, to have open-heart surgery.

"Let's do it," Hearn said.

With three simple words, he thus ended a consecutive-game streak that stretched over four decades. On Wednesday, December 19, 2001, Dr. Michael Soltero performed open-heart surgery on the 85-year-old announcer at Northridge Hospital Medical Center.

PAUL SUNDERLAND
Hearn's Successor

I was at home, locked up in my office, preparing to go into a voiceover studio the next day for an NBC project. There was a lot of preparation involved, and I was just plowing away.

My phone rang. It was a reporter who asked, "Have you heard about Chick?" I told him I had no comment because he had caught me off guard. I didn't know what he was talking about. I immediately put in a call to [Lakers public relations director] John Black. In the meantime, I turned on the radio and TV and learned Chick was facing heart surgery.

John called back and, before I could even ask him anything, he said, "Here, hold on for Mitch [Kupchak]." Mitch asked me I if would be willing and able to fill in for Chick, beginning with a game the next night in Houston. He told me they were considering three or four people.

I said, "Of course, I'd be willing. I'd be able."

At that point, everybody knew it was going to be for more than one game. How many? Who knew?

I still had this commitment to NBC, which was not the Lakers' concern. I called network officials in New York, and they told me they already knew Chick had been taken ill and they figured I'd be a strong possibility to fill in.

Mitch called back and said, "We've taken our list of names to Dr. Buss, and we want you to do the game."

I went into the studio and did my voiceover at 3:00 in the morning, finished about 7:00, got on a plane for Houston, and did the game that night.

It really wasn't a job I had ever thought of. Not only was I doing the Laker pregame show at the time, but I was also doing a lot of NBA play-by-play for NBC. People saw that and would ask me about the Laker play-by-play job. But I just didn't see myself in that position and I think it was because of Chick. I've lived in L.A. all my life. I've been a Laker fan as long as I can remember, and I couldn't imagine Chick not doing the games.

I thought, in the natural evolution of my career, I'd go off and work for Portland or San Antonio or Milwaukee. And I'd keep doing the NBA on NBC or Turner.

That first night, I wasn't trying to make an impression. I was trying to survive.

The first game I did at Staples Center was on Christmas Day. The broadcast area was set up. I asked one of the ushers, "Is this Chick's chair?"

"Well," he said, "that's where Chick sits."

"No, no, you don't understand," I insisted. "Is that Chick's *chair?*"

"Well, yeah."

"You've got to get me another one," I said, trying not to appear snooty. "I am not going to sit in Chick's chair. Because he's coming back."

So they took the chair away and brought me another one.

And even after I filled in for Chick on those 56 games, even then, I never thought I'd have the job. I really didn't.

I thought I had filled in, I had done the best I could, but Chick was back.

Lon Rosen
Sports Agent

About three or four days after Chick's heart surgery, I went to see him with Jerry West. Chick was still in intensive care at the time.

He was just coming around, a little slow, but he was still Chick.

He asked me to come real close, pulled me up to him, and said, "Lonnie, you make sure, until I'm better, they don't take away my job."

Jerry Buss
Laker Owner

Chick was already older when I got there. I figured it was going to be such a tough job to replace him that it was going to take at least a two-year search. This was in my fourth or fifth year, in the early eighties. So, I said to Bob Steiner, "Why don't we get tapes on everybody?"

We selected some people who were very good. The problem was, they got old and retired, and Chick was still here.

It was a miracle to us that he could still call games at his age.

I don't think he would have ever retired. I think we may have been able to talk him into not going on the road. But in terms of not doing the home games, there was no way. Absolutely none.

BOB STEINER
Public Relations Director for California Sports

In the early eighties, we were thinking that Chick couldn't go on forever.

Although he came close.

Jerry Buss told me to listen to other announcers and see if I had any recommendations for an eventual successor. So for a long time, I sat up where Chick did, but next to the visiting team's announcers. You hear a bunch of people who are good compared to their competition but not good compared to Chick.

I came back to Jerry and told him that.

Nothing happened, of course, and then, a couple of years ago, Jerry asked me to look around again. This time, I solicited some tapes and some recommendations from [NBA Senior Vice President] Brian McIntyre and other people around the league. We heard a lot of good announcers, but they weren't Chick. And therein lay the problem: finding the guy to replace Chick.

———

It became increasingly difficult for Chick to be Chick as the years rolled by.

J. A. ADANDE
Los Angeles Times Columnist

In his later years, he would come into the press room to eat before the game, and that's when he would show his age. You would think, "Wow, this is your grandfather. This is an old guy." But then he'd go upstairs and that red camera light would come on, and boom, showtime. I don't know where all that energy came from. But from 7:00 to 10:00 every game night, he was the Chick Hearn we know and remember. That was the one thing that never waned.

SHAQUILLE O'NEAL
Laker Center
Every now and then, he slipped up on a name. One time, he called me Shaquille Alcindor. That was just telling me he saw some of them in me.

RICK FOX
Laker Forward
He would get so into the game that he would mix generations of players, and do it so convincingly that you actually looked on the floor for that player.

LARRY STEWART
Los Angeles Times Media Critic
As the radio-TV columnist for the *Times*, I was always asking Chick about retirement. And he would always come up with something different. He once said he would retire when Magic retired. Then, of course, Magic became HIV positive and had to retire, and Chick came up with a reason why he wasn't ready to do the same. He always had an excuse.

I really thought he might consider announcing his retirement after the Lakers won their third straight championship. I sat with Marge for the entire second half of the final game. We both thought it would be ideal if Chick said, at the end of the broadcast, that the next season would be his last. He could have a farewell tour.

He didn't, of course, mention retirement at the end of that broadcast. I went over to his house anyway after the season to talk about the subject. I even told my sports editor, Bill Dwyre, that I might come back with the story of Chick's retirement. "No," insisted Dwyre, "he is not going to announce it."

When I got to Chick's Encino home, I asked him, "Have you thought about announcing your retirement after next season?"

"That's what Marge wants me to do," Chick said, "but I'm not ready to make that announcement."

"You are never going to be able to make that announcement," I told him.

"You're right," Chick said. "What if I was to announce my retirement and then I decide I don't want to do that?"

He was just driven. The Lakers were his life. He said to me a couple of times, "If I were to retire, I would not live long after that."

MARY LOU LIEBICH
Laker Administrative Assistant

The move from the Forum to Staples was a big change for Chick. He no longer had an office. The whole atmosphere was different. At the Forum, it was a family atmosphere. At Staples, it's a business atmosphere. I think it bothered him.

But still, I couldn't envision him retiring. I don't think he could have handled it. I really don't. This was just his whole life. As soon as a season ended, he was ready to get started on the next one.

MITCH KUPCHAK
Laker Player and General Manager

When I moved into the front office to work with Jerry West in 1986, we would talk about Chick and when he was going to retire. More accurately, *if* he was going to retire.

At times, as he advanced in age, you wondered, my goodness, is it something he should consider? But to us, ultimately, it was a foregone conclusion that he really wasn't going to retire.

PAT RILEY
Former Laker Player, Broadcast Analyst, Assistant Coach, and Coach

Retirement? No way. Chick loved it too much. What was he going to do? Commercials? Voiceovers? He was the greatest NBA broadcaster ever. You are who you are by nature.

J. A. ADANDE

Those thirty-three-hundred-plus games, and he never lost his enthusiasm. I don't think I'll ever love anything as much as Chick loved his job. How many people get to experience that? The only way he was going to leave that chair was the way he did.

"HOT" ROD HUNDLEY
Former Laker Player and Broadcast Analyst

I knew he was never going to quit, that he was going to die with a mike in his hand.

Marge said to me once, "When Chick retires, the Lakers should give you his job."

I told her, "I'll retire before he does."

She said, "You're probably right."

ROY FIRESTONE
National Sportscaster Who also Did a Lakers Pregame Show from 1985–1991

I don't believe he would have lasted long without the Lakers. The Lakers kept him alive, kept him thriving, kept him from the horror of life. I don't see how the man could have survived without them.

———

Following his heart surgery, Hearn was determined to not only survive, but to return to the broadcast perch that had long been his home. He worked diligently through the holidays, through January and into February, circling March 1, a home game against the Indiana Pacers, as the date of his return.

But on Sunday night, February 17, after watching in despair on television as the Lakers were defeated by the Trail Blazers in Portland, Chick took Marge out to dinner. Marge had already made dinner at home, but Chick told her he was so upset by the loss that he needed to get out.

Stopping at a service station at the corner of Ventura and Balboa in the San Fernando Valley for gas, he stepped out to man the gas pump, but the car started rolling.

Marge, in the passenger seat, yelled out to Chick while reaching over and turning off the ignition. But the car kept moving.

Chick tried to hop back in, but the door hit him, knocking him to the pavement. The car slid into a shrub, preventing it from rolling into the street.

Marge looked back and saw Chick stretched out on the ground.

"I think I broke my hip," he yelled.

Susan Stratton
He tried so hard to come back and then broke the hip. It was the only time I ever heard Marge cry.

Bill Sharman
Laker Coach and Front-Office Executive
You just never knew what Chick was going to say. When he was in the hospital preparing for his hip-replacement surgery, Marge, standing by his bed, asked if he needed anything.

"Just be sure and tell that silly doctor," he said, "not to sew my leg on backward."

Hearn's unsinkable sense of humor hadn't deserted him even in the face of yet another setback. As he was being wheeled in for the hip surgery, a doctor said, "Chick, at your age, why are you still pumping your own gas?"

Without pause, Hearn snapped back, "So I can afford to pay you."

The double whammy—heart surgery and hip-replacement surgery in a span of two months—seemed too much for even Hearn to overcome. But on April 9, less than two months after the fall, he gingerly settled into his old broadcast chair at Staples Center, the one Sunderland refused to sit in, and invited the audience to listen to the Lakers and the Utah Jazz.

STU LANTZ
Laker Broadcast Analyst

After the hip replacement, he showed a lot of gumption. They wanted him to use a wheelchair to get to the airport or wherever we were going.

When the Grizzlies were still in Vancouver, we had to walk to customs at the Vancouver airport, which was a long way from where we had parked our plane. And then we had to get to our buses. That was another long walk. At that point, Chick's knee was bad. So he agreed to take a wheelchair, but that hurt his pride.

So when he had the hip replacement and they wanted him to use a wheelchair, he wouldn't do it. He had a walker, but he had worked so hard on his rehab that he didn't even want to use the walker. That's the pride he had in his ability to continue to do his job, even at 85.

GARY VITTI
Laker Trainer

How could you not be amazed at him?

RICK FOX

I thought we had lost him to the heart ailment and the hip injury. But to be back doing the games and traveling with us, it was really an example of mind over matter, an example of, when you love something, how far you'll go to be a part of it.

LARRY BURNETT
L.A. Radio Host
Just before he came back from the hip surgery, I did an interview with him at his home. He related to me how much doing his job meant to him, and how much he loved the fans loving the fact he was coming back.

PAT O'BRIEN
National Television Host
The year Chick died, I had a friend who knew somebody whose kid was dying. All the kid wanted to do was meet Chick Hearn. So I called Chick and asked him if he could spend some time at halftime with this kid. He said sure. I brought the kid up and it changed his life for the moment. His sick world stopped and he was almost healthy.

It couldn't last. A couple of weeks later, the kid died, but before he did, he had told his parents that the coolest moment of his life was the moment he met Chick Hearn.

————

Bidding for a third straight championship, the Lakers went through Portland, San Antonio, Sacramento, and finally New Jersey in the postseason, with Hearn again along for the ride. On June 12, at Continental Airlines Arena, the Lakers completed a sweep of the New Jersey Nets in the NBA Finals with a 113–107 victory.

SUSAN STRATTON
I was in New Jersey doing the high-definition feed for Japanese television. I got them to bring Chick and Stu's feed into the truck so that I could hear them and then go out and criticize them.

Which I didn't, of course. There was nothing to criticize.

As the buzzer sounded and the players embraced and the Laker fans in attendance roared, there was Hearn, describing the celebration, as he had done for the previous eight titles the team had won in L.A.

STEVE LOMBARDO
Laker Team Doctor

Chick beat all the statistics. I've talked to a lot of specialists and, for a person to have that hip fracture at his age, the chances of him surviving for a year were very, very small. It takes a lot out of an older person to have something like that.

Then to come back and travel to New Jersey like he did caused us concern. Mitch [Kupchak] arranged for a therapist to go with Chick. But he was like an elephant with gnats buzzing around him. He kept telling us he was fine. It was just unbelievable.

When a person sets their mind to something, when they have a passion for it, nothing is going to stop them. Nothing was going to stop Chick from coming back.

SUSAN STRATTON

The fact that he came back for the end of the season was incredible, the most fabulous thing that could have happened.

I have to admit it worried me a lot because I thought it was too much for him, frankly. The travel and the pressure are enormous. He had fallen a number of times. His footing was very insecure. The arena floors stick up, there are a number of uneven surfaces, and there's cable all over hell and gone. It's hard. Marge was with him, and he also had a trainer and a therapist, yet I still worried about him.

But he lived on it. It was his lifeblood. I don't know what he would have done if he couldn't do that.

God gave him a gift in the form of those final games. He said, here, this is for you. I was so thrilled for him and Marge. That he could do that.

That he could have that. How many people in their lives have that, have their career finish that way?

MITCH KUPCHAK

The Lakers became the thing he lived for. It was real important for him to come back.

The most important thing is, a comeback became a goal to get him through his surgery. He was able to pinpoint a certain time when he was going to be able to get back and work. I think that helped him in his recovery.

When he did make it back, he was so grateful, so happy to complete the season and announce yet another championship.

STEVE CHASE
Laker Fantasy Camp Operator

Jerry Buss and I started a Laker postseason fantasy camp 20 years ago when he still owned the Ocotillo Lodge in Palm Springs. Because it was 120 degrees there in the summertime, he couldn't give rooms away. The idea was, people who came to the camp would be exposed to the hotel. Then, for 13 years, we held the camp in Hawaii.

A lot of players were involved, from Jerry West to Magic Johnson. Kurt Rambis had been there from day one. We'd have 30 adult campers, and, at the end of the four-day session, we would play a game in front of a camera with Chick doing the play-by-play. The campers would receive a video of the broadcast, a treasured memento. Chick treated it and prepared for it the way he prepared for an NBA game, learning about the players and incorporating that information into the broadcast.

When Chick had all his health problems, I thought it could be the end of the camp, which had been moved to Las Vegas.

I called Chick just to see how he was doing. "Hey, Stevo," he said. "You still doing the camp this year?" I was honestly just calling to see how he felt, but he brought the camp up before I had a chance to talk. He loved Vegas and he loved the guys in the camp. It was a labor of love.

I offered to send a car for him, but he wanted to drive there with Marge. When he got to Las Vegas, he was in good spirits, looking healthy. He didn't even have a noticeable limp from the hip surgery. He and Marge went to dinner, to the shows, and got in some gambling. He even came to practice and did some preparation for the broadcast.

Since the third or fourth year of the camp, I had done the color commentating on the broadcast. Fifty percent of the reason I wanted to keep the camp going was because I wanted to still be Chick's commentator for one day a year.

Unfortunately, as it turned out, I was the last commentator to work with Chick.

Every year, he would end the broadcast by saying, "For Steve Chase, this is Chick Hearn once again reminding you the final score is blah, blah, and here's hoping we can all be together here again next year." And then, he would say, "Good afternoon," or, "Good night."

But this time, he said, "This is Chick Hearn saying good-bye." He said it with a crack in his voice like he knew it was good-bye.

It sent a chill down my spine. I wanted to say we should go back and redo it, but who the hell am I to tell Chick Hearn to redo a broadcast? It didn't sit well with me, but I let it go.

MARGE HEARN

He would never say good-bye. He had a thing against it, wouldn't do it. He thought good-bye was too final.

LINDA RAMBIS
Kurt Rambis' Wife and a Member of the Laker Front-Office Staff

Chick was enjoying himself immensely at the camp. We all went out to a Chinese restaurant and then a nightclub the last night. Marge and Chick had a few drinks. Marge was playing her slot machines and Chick was following her around.

I really think he and Marge enjoyed themselves on that trip. I really think, right up to the last moment, he was a vibrant person, enjoying his connection to this team.

———

Chick and Marge stayed in Las Vegas an extra day to celebrate Marge's birthday, then came home on a Thursday.

MARGE HEARN

We were sitting out in the backyard by the pool late Friday afternoon. Fran, who loved his gardening, pointed to a plant. "It should be turned around to the other side," he said. "It's not getting any sun."

"Let the gardener do it," I told him.

I never thought another thing about it. I got up to take something out for dinner and asked him if he was coming in. He said, "I'll be right there."

I have no idea what drove me to go back out there. I must have heard the noise of the pot that held the plant shattering. I saw the pieces at the bottom of the steps leading to our pool.

And lying on the pool deck was Fran. He must have tried to turn the plant himself and fallen, his head hitting the concrete. If he'd tumbled any further, he'd have gone into the water.

He couldn't have been lying there long. I screamed at him, but got no response. I shook him, jolted him, trying to get any reaction, but there was none. His eyes didn't look good. When he fell backward, he picked up momentum. He must have hit awfully hard.

Unable to get through to 911, I called my neighbor, Sandy Kessler, who said she'd take care of it. I grabbed a pillow, put it under Fran's head, and covered him with a blanket. I always heard it was good to cover somebody up in a situation like that. I didn't know what else I could do.

Chick

SANDY KESSLER
A Hearn Neighbor

It was September of 1973 when the new neighbors moved in. How should I act? After all, it's a celebrity.

Finally, I decided to do what was done for me three and a half years earlier when my family and I moved into the neighborhood. I would offer a welcome. I waited until midmorning, knowing I'd be greeted by a maid or the lady of the house. Certainly not by the celebrity himself.

I came over about 10:00 A.M., piece of paper in hand, and knocked on the door. Much to my surprise, it was opened by this 6'3" handsome hunk in bathing trunks and a robe.

It was Chick Hearn.

What do I do now?

I stammered and stuttered, finally getting out the words. "Hi, I'm Sandy Kessler, your neighbor, kitty corner from you," I said. "I'd like to give you my name and phone number in case you need anything while you're settling in."

I took a deep breath but was immediately put at ease by Chick's response.

"Thanks so much," he said. "Wait a minute and I'll write down our number so you'll have it. See, I travel a lot and it will be a great comfort to me to know that my wife, Marge, will have an emergency number if I'm not around."

It was the beginning of a long and meaningful friendship—heartfelt comfort at times of need both ways (Hearns to Kesslers, Kesslers to Hearns), rejoicing at Shannon's wedding, the birth of Kayla, the broken sprinkler, the garage door left open, suspicious cars on the block, calls back and forth between the two households—that stretched over 30 years.

Then, August 2, 2002, a call of sheer panic. I instantly recognized Marge's voice.

"Sandy," she said, "Fran fell in the yard and I keep calling 911 and getting a busy signal."

"Marge, hang up," I said. "I'll take care of it."

I called 911, then went across the street to wait with Marge until the paramedics arrived.

When they put Chick, in his bathing trunks and robe, on a gurney, I leaned over and said, "Hang in there. We love you."

I keep reliving that night, thinking about my neighbor, my friend. I met him in his bathing trunks and robe, and I said good-bye to him in his bathing trunks and robe.

———

Taken to Northridge Hospital Medical Center, the same place where he had his open-heart surgery nearly eight months before, Hearn underwent two craniotomies to control brain hemorrhaging, but he remained in critical condition as the weekend dragged on.

When Marge came home Saturday night to get some rest, she kept playing his fall over and over in her head.

MARGE HEARN

When that season ended, all his surgeries behind him, he was feeling better than he had in three years. It's sad to have gotten through all those serious things and then to take that stupid fall because of a plant. But that's the way it was.

Everybody's career must end sometime. But if he could have lived a normal life after that, we could have handled that. I didn't care about the games. But all that was out of our control.

I went into intensive care and spoke to Fran, but I don't know if he ever heard me.

BOB STEINER

Marge showed such strength throughout the ordeal. The only thing that scared her was that Chick would suffer. That was the thing she was most in dread about. The doctors assured her that wasn't going to be the case.

From among the thousands of calls and cards coming into the hospital, Marge was handed a get-well card from a young child who had drawn several eggs hatching with the idea that a healthy chick would emerge.

Instead, Chick Hearn died on August 5, 2002. He was 85.

STEVE CHASE

The first thing I thought of when I heard the news was that the last word Chick would ever say on a mike was good-bye.

CURT SANDOVAL
L.A. Sportscaster

Within what seemed like seconds of the announcement at Northridge Hospital that Chick had died, people started showing up to leave flowers.

After a few hours, I went over to look at the display and I saw that one fan had left some eggs, some butter, and a little transistor radio, along with a note that simply read, "Thanks, Chick."

HOWARD BECK
Laker Beat Writer for the *Los Angeles Daily News*

I grew up in the Bay area, so the Lakers were just that team down south. I didn't have that emotional attachment to Chick. It came from covering the beat for several years while he was the announcer. I grew to respect and love the guy a lot. And I really felt it when he died.

That weekend, listening to the radio, talking to people, you understood the way they felt about him. If you didn't know before how big Chick was in this city, as beloved as Magic, as beloved as Jerry West, you knew it then. You understood at that moment when people started to realize, "Oh my God, we may lose this guy. We may lose Chick Hearn."

That Monday, when the call finally came that he was gone, I started working on the story, the story I did not want to have to write. I begged my editors to allow me to avoid it, but I couldn't. It was tough to write a story like that about someone you knew and had great affection for.

I turned on the radio in the background so I could hear the fans on talk radio. Every single person who called in was not only talking about how much they loved the guy, how great he was, how he taught them basketball, but it sounded like every single one of them had met him at some point. Every person had a story to tell about the time he took his picture with them, the time he gave them an autograph, whatever. It was as if Chick had met all 10 million people in the greater Los Angeles area at some point in the last 40 years.

That was the great thing about him. He was this icon and yet so accessible, so much a man of the people.

———

With an entire city in mourning, a monumental task still lay ahead: planning a funeral worthy of this man of the people.

Spearheaded by Jeanie Buss, the task was accomplished with a day that offered something for everyone. There was a private service at St. Martin of Tours Church in Brentwood, attended by everyone from California governor Gray Davis and Los Angeles mayor James Hahn to Jack Nicholson, Vin Scully, and Lakers spanning every era included in Hearn's word's-eye view.

There was a tribute at Staples Center where the public was invited in free to pay their respects at Hearn's broadcast perch. An estimated eighteen thousand people filed by.

And there was television coverage of the funeral, with every station in Los Angeles showing it live from beginning to end, an unprecedented honor never before afforded to a resident of the city—not politicians nor movie stars nor sports heroes.

BOB STEINER

Cardinal Roger Mahony called and wanted to officiate. The governor called and wanted to come. It couldn't be an open funeral. It just couldn't.

211

You would have to turn down too many people. You are not going to do a funeral in the Coliseum.

Jeanie stepped up big time, working with the church and getting the Staples Center involved so that people could come and pay their respects. And the setting up of his broadcast spot was tremendous.

LINDA RAMBIS

Jeanie had no experience doing something like this, but she did have the sense to realize the fans were going to feel this loss tremendously. She knew there had to be a way for our fans to grieve together with the team, all the people who appreciated the life Chick had breathed into our games.

And Jeanie did that all herself. I was nowhere to be found to help her. Kurt and I and our family were in Hawaii and her father was in Europe. So it was a really difficult time, but Jeanie had really great instincts.

She also took care of Marge, who, of course, was devastated.

JEANIE BUSS
Laker Executive Vice President of Business Operations

I never thought I would be involved in such a sad event for me and my family. It was during the summer, which meant my father was in Europe, Phil [Jackson] was in Montana, Linda Rambis, who works so closely with me, was in Hawaii, and John Black was in the hospital for heart surgery.

You do what you have to do. I knew we could never, ever, ever, ever do enough for what Chick meant to this team and my family. But whatever we were going to do, we had to make decisions quickly.

We knew it was important that the Hearn family have an intimate ceremony. We wanted something that would be full of dignity and connection.

We also knew there would be such a demand for public participation. And if we didn't satisfy that demand, the private family ceremony would be overrun. You had fans who would not stay away. You had to give people the opportunity for closure, the opportunity to take care of their feelings.

The Staples Center people offered their building to us with open arms. We set up Chick's nest exactly as if he were calling a game. We turned off all the lights in the arena except for a spotlight on his empty chair. We had welcome books for the fans to sign to share their feelings.

Some of our people were worried. How are the fans going to react? Will it get out of hand? But every person who made the effort to get to Staples Center that day was quiet and respectful.

I don't know what would have happened without Bob Steiner, someone who just seemed to know all the right things to do. So many others contributed as well. Tim Harris, the Lakers' senior vice president of business, was amazing. There was our great game-operations department, Michael Roth, Tim Leiweke, Lee Zeidman, Ian Levitt, all the people from Staples Center. They all said, "What do you want us to do? What do you need us to do?" And they did it. I never heard "no" as an answer.

With the amount of grief everybody felt, they all wanted to roll up their sleeves and do something. You think of all the people you'd want to be with in that situation, and it ended up being all the people we had. My life changed because of that in knowing who I could always count on.

Marge was so strong and so amazing. When I thought I would fall apart, I just went up to her and I knew we could get through this.

SHAQUILLE O'NEAL

A lot of people are probably still upset I didn't attend the funeral. But I had my own problems at that time, personal problems that I can't really talk about. It was something big or I would have been there.

Besides, I'm not really good with funerals. I don't want my last vision of Chick Hearn to be laying there like that. Instead, my last vision is of him talking to me.

If people are mad at me, I'm sorry.

It's kind of weird without him around, but he lived an excellent life, a great life. And he's in a better place now.

His wife, Marge, still beautiful, has done an unbelievable job of keeping his memory alive.

MITCH KUPCHAK

I don't think Marge gets enough credit. She was really an incredible source of strength and humor for Chick. I think a lot of people didn't understand that, didn't realize it. But I think they have seen it more now that he is gone.

ALAN MASSENGALE
L.A. Sportscaster

Right after Chick dies, we get a phone call at KHJ. The receptionist phones my producer upstairs, Mike Muriano, and says, "There's a guy on the line says he's Jack Nicholson."

Mike says, "Ye-a-ah, sure, put him through."

Sure enough, the guy sounds like Jack Nicholson.

Mike's thinking, "Everybody does Jack Nicholson."

The caller hangs up and Jack's publicist calls back and says it was Jack and he feels like he needs to make a statement about the death of Chick Hearn and wonders if we could arrange something.

Mike is still not sure if this is on the level or we're getting jacked around, because Jack Nicholson doesn't do interviews. And he certainly doesn't call TV stations. I tell Mike, call back and tell him we'll come out there, and ask if it's such-and-such an address because I know where Jack lives.

Sure enough, that's the address and they convince him it would be better if he went on camera rather than just issuing a statement.

So I go up there sweating—and I don't normally get nervous on interviews—I get to the address, pull in the gate, and I think I'm going to see a publicist. Jack's going to come out, say something, and leave. Because he's Jack.

Instead, as I come up the driveway, Jack himself comes out in very casual attire. I roll down my window, and he sticks his head into my car and says, "Hi, Al, glad you could make it."

His face is about six inches from mine, and all I can think of, with all the great movies he's done from *Chinatown* to *The Shining*, is that the Joker's got his face in my car.

He tells me that the reason he called Channel 9, the Lakers' local station for a quarter century, is that he felt that is what Chick would have wanted. He says, "I know a lot of other stations may be mad at me, but this is why I came to you guys."

Now you can't ask regular questions of Jack because he already knows what he wants to say. He tells me, "Nothing ever galvanized Los Angeles like Chick Hearn, except for an earthquake."

He also tells me it was the first time his young son understood what death was because he asked Jack, "Is Chick all the way dead?"

He says he remembered when Franklin Roosevelt died, my generation remembers when John Kennedy died, and this generation of Los Angelinos will remember when Chick Hearn died. Jack felt it was that big.

He does a great interview, he speaks from the heart, and he speaks for the fans of Los Angeles. And he wants to make sure it's right because this was the only interview he was going to do.

Now in local television, especially on short notice, we only have one camera to work with, so we have to do what we call reverse shots. After we have shown the interview subject, we turn around and re-create the interviewer asking the questions.

When we are done with the formal interview, Jack says to me, "Are you going to do that edit shot?" I told him we were and he says, "Let me tell you what we're going to do here. You say this and I'll start the answer. It will look great."

And I'm thinking, "Jack Nicholson is directing me." It was a beautiful moment.

JOEL GLASS
Orlando Magic Media Relations Director

We send out a survey in the off-season with a self-addressed envelope to the media, asking them to grade our performance. I got a response from Chick. Rather than filling the survey out, he had simply written across the top: "Joel, you and your staff do a great job. Thanks for everything, Chick Hearn."

I was shocked that he would take the time. Who am I that Chick Hearn needs to be writing me a note? I guess that was just the kind of person he was.

What was eerie was that I received the note two days after he had died. It must have been one of the last things he wrote.

Lucius Allen
Former Laker

In a letter to Marge upon Chick's death:

> Words can't fill the void I am experiencing, so I won't try. He was a dear friend of mine. When I needed his help after my retirement, he couldn't say yes fast enough.

Steve Lombardo

A guy like Magic joins the team, the team starts winning, and you just take it for granted that's the way it is. You appreciate him for his value to himself, to the team, and to the public.

But once a person like that leaves, you appreciate him 10 times more.

Chick was the same way. He will never be replaced. I appreciated him for what he did then—I'm into history—what he did for the team and for basketball. But I appreciate him even more now.

Dyan Cannon
Actress

It's not the same. It's like a car without an engine. He's irreplaceable. You've heard songs like that. His enthusiasm, his knowledge, all the sayings he invented. How many people are there like that in the world?

Brian Golden
Antelope Valley Press Columnist

Chick was the voice of basketball, teaching the game to several generations in L.A., but maybe his greatest gift was simply being himself, having this remarkable ability to seemingly defy the aging process. It just didn't seem to affect him. He got a pass, like Michael Jordan got a pass from the rules of physics and gravity.

That was a very reassuring thing. Because no matter what ravages of time were occurring in your own life, whether physically or otherwise, Chick Hearn on the radio was a constant that was very comforting.

I remember one night he had a raspy voice, making things seem a little bit out of kilter, but it was still Chick. He was always there. God bless people like that. I looked at someone like him and said, "There's hope."

That's why I think his death hit people with such a devastating impact.

LARRY BURNETT

Chick had these spotting charts that were on these little bitty cut pieces of cardboard. They were so small, I couldn't read them. But he could at 85. They were all carefully handwritten. He had a black pen for this and a red pen for that.

I kept saying that I wanted to get him to sign one for me so I could take it home and have it. I never did. I *never* did. And then he passed away.

———

On the first Valentine's Day after Chick's death, Rick Fox sent flowers to Marge.

RICK FOX

I'm sure it is a tough time in anybody's life when you are not with your loved one on that special day. I was just thinking about her.

DEREK FISHER
Laker Guard

Whenever somebody who has been a staple of an organization moves on, or has gone to a better place, there is something that leaves with that person. I think we all have to recognize that there is a different type of energy without Chick being around. After winning three championships and Chick being a part of that, we lost him over that summer. What happened? The next season turned out to be tumultuous, and we didn't win the championship.

Everything is connected. He was a part of our team, our organization. It was just like losing a key player. He brought energy, he brought people to support us and feel good about the Lakers.

Losing him took a lot of people down to a different place, a place of low energy. Fans were down. Maybe they couldn't push us over the hump in some games where we really needed them. With Chick there, maybe they would have been screaming louder and really pushing us to come back.

Stu Lantz

I think of Chick just about any time I think of the Lakers, just about any time I set foot in the Chick Hearn Press Room at Staples Center.

I always keep his press pass with me. It never comes out of my wallet, so he's with me all the time. People will come up to me at games and they just want to talk about Chick.

You can't forget him.

You just can't, especially when you think of basketball and the Lakers. Chick and the Lakers are synonymous.

Curt Sandoval

Being a broadcast guy, I still keep the card from his funeral in my wallet as a reminder of his dedication.

Jeanie Buss

The organization has split the broadcasts into radio and television. No simulcasts, which really makes sense. It's the right decision. But, thinking of Chick, it was hard to let that go.

JOHN IRELAND
L.A. Sportscaster

Two seasons after Chick had died, I was down on the floor at a Laker game in Phoenix to do courtside interviews. Paul Sunderland told the audience, "Let's go to John Ireland, who is standing by with a special guest."

I said, "Thanks, Paul. I'm here with Charles Barkley."

Before I could ask a question, Barkley said, on the air, "Is that Paul Sunderland?"

I said, "Yeah."

"Well tell him he's no Chick Hearn."

Caught off guard, I responded, "Well, he'd be the first to tell you that."

"I miss Chick Hearn," repeated Barkley.

I couldn't get him to stop talking about Chick. I felt bad for Paul, but Paul later said he certainly understood.

That just shows you the reaction Chick continues to get.

PAUL SUNDERLAND

Chick was the best in the business for *four* decades. That's how he carved out his identity. Anybody who thought they could carve out an identity in 1 game or 56 games or two years or three years or five years is barking up the wrong tree.

People introduce me as the guy who replaced Chick. Nobody replaces Chick. I succeeded him because he's no longer with us. I'll never be Chick. Nobody will ever be Chick. If anybody tries, then they are not being themselves. You have to have the confidence to be yourself. That's all I've ever tried to do.

And I've gotten a lot of support. I got a lot of support from Chick when I first filled in. He was incredibly supportive. So was Marge.

I can't imagine doing this for 42 years. That's just not me from where I'm sitting. Ask me in 10 years and maybe I'll be like Chick. Two days after the season, I'll be bitching because the off-season is too long.

JEANIE BUSS

I don't think I've recovered from Chick's death yet. The Lakers are going to go on and win more championships, and there are going to be so many great moments to come. But it's never going to be the same.

———

The Lakers will win many games in the future, but never again will they put one in the refrigerator. Because the door is shut, the light's out, and that wonderful, inspiring voice is forever stilled.

Afterword

It was in 1962 that I, as a kid in San Diego, first discovered this brilliant historian, journalist, comedian, and actor who used basketball and the NBA as his stage.

Growing up in a nonathletic household without a television set, my imagination was driven by books, newspapers, and my small, handheld transistor radio. As I collapsed into bed at night—my dreams of seemingly endless games to play having been fulfilled—I convinced my parents that I was, indeed, packing it in for the evening.

Little did they know that is when the real action began for me. Under the covers, under the pillow, it was the beginning of my most exciting love affair. And I was only 10 years old.

Chick and me. What could ever be better?

I had no idea where this would all lead. I had no concept that, for me, the games would go on forever. And I certainly had no comprehension of the impact that special voice on the other end of that radio would have on my life.

Chick Hearn taught me how to play basketball. He also taught me how to think about the game, ultimately showing me how to love a world that would become my life.

Or so I thought. It wasn't until the years started to add up and I began to learn all the things I was so sure I already knew that I realized Chick was teaching me the game of life the whole time.

There was nothing like growing up with the comforting thought that Chick was your best friend, knowing that, at the end of the day, he would be there with more. The creativity, the excitement, the intensity, the exuberance, the vibrancy, the honesty, the personal touch were all delivered in a way that convinced me that he was speaking directly to me. Like any best friend, Chick was always about you. He never asked, he always gave.

He was the perfect artist who could take the dark out of the nighttime.

From the beginning, Chick was able to deliver peak performances on command, somehow always rising, never dropping, always at his best. He was so good, made you feel so at ease, it was as if he was your dad. It always seemed so simple, so effortless, belying the eternity that he spent selflessly perfecting himself for me.

My best friend was a pillar of strength and stability who carried the weight of the world on his immense shoulders. Chick always stood erect, proud, and true in the face of the most extreme adversity and devastating personal tragedy. He never gave anyone the sense the universe wasn't in perfect harmony. Chick gave all of us everything that he had. He never held back, never looked back.

To me, it still seems like yesterday, still under the pillow with the transistor. No one has ever given us more. That is what best friends are all about.

Yet more is all I have wanted since the day he died, my first lonely day in over 40 years.

—Bill Walton
Player and Broadcaster